THE
STRATEGY
MINDSET

DR. CHUCK BAMFORD

A PRACTICAL GUIDE TO THE
DESIGN AND IMPLEMENTATION
OF STRATEGY

ISBN: 1505443059

ISBN 13: 9781505443059

Library of Congress Control Number: 2014921984

CreateSpace Independent Publishing Platform

North Charleston, South Carolina

CONTENTS

INTRODUCTION

There are many strategy books on the market. Most are textbooks that are really designed as a support to classroom lectures and an aid for the uninitiated to the world of business at the executive level. For the practically oriented business executive, they are thick, mind-numbing reads (because they are not meant to be read like a book) that are five-hundred-plus pages of text with thousands of citations and a $200-plus price point. I know; I've written a few.

There are also so-called strategy books written by famous CEOs who try to share the wisdom they think they found while running a particular company. Some of these provide an interesting insight into history, but only a rare few (and they are remarkable) provide any clue as to the application of strategy at another company in another time and place.

Then there are the vast array of books written by people with little or no real understanding of strategy who have decided to anoint themselves with the title "strategy consultant" and apply their wizardry (often with ridiculous titles meant to ensure years of sales) to the masses. They spell out some vague multistep (putting it in terms of numbers seems to be in vogue—Ten Things or Eight Paths) approach that they are sure will work and try to develop a cult following of their preaching. I've read many of these in a vain attempt to keep ahead of executives asking me if I've read this or that great book. They are simply a waste of time.

So, in that vein, one may legitimately ask, why consider another book on this subject?

Businesses are terrible at strategy! Executives don't understand it. They think it is some type of witchcraft or mental endowment with which one proves one's manhood or womanhood, or they simply throw up their hands and surrender to SWOT! Please, if you get nothing from this book, or if you read this opening and decide not to read any further, do one thing for your company—*never* use SWOT as a strategy approach again. That alone should help the bottom line.

Strategy has most of its written roots in Sun Tzu's *The Art of War* and a long history of military application that was loosely translated into business. Those crude translations worked well while the logistic ability to reach new customers was expanding rapidly, conglomerates were seen as the epitome of effectiveness, and company growth was assured in a rapidly growing economy.

All of that started falling apart in the 1970s. It was probably falling apart before then, but the fallout from the OPEC-inspired energy embargos, the ending of the Vietnam War, and the introduction of the personal computer meant that strategy no longer followed the command-and-control, conquer-and-succeed strategy models that had been in vogue for so long. A famous line used over and over is that soldiers are trained to kill anything that comes over the hill, not nimbly assess changing conditions and shoot judiciously.

Business strategy had to start focusing on why customers *really* buy a product or service from a company and what distinguishes that company in the eye of the customer. Strategy had to be designed and crafted for the real needs and wants of customer groups.

Business strategy is at best 50 percent science and 50 percent art. It is probably more like 35 percent science and 65 percent art, but there is a science. There is a process that works. If done with some rigor, applying the science of strategy will separate your company from all your competitors and allow you to earn extraordinary returns.

I don't say this lightly. As a corporate guy in the 1980s and early 1990s, I was continually frustrated with our organization's inability to move beyond the superficial talk about how our employees were our competitive advantage or how our dedication to quality, efficiency, customer service, or any of the other pop approaches of the day would lead to extraordinary returns. In general, customers couldn't care less whom you employ as long as the company delivers. Customers are indifferent to your efficiency; they know that every company claims that quality is job number one, and they are immune to the preachings about how customer service is the centerpiece of the company. They know that customer service is not the centerpiece of your strategy, or you would behave differently to customers!

These are all well-intentioned and, in most cases, totally believed strategies. I will discuss all these myths in the first chapter (including the farce that SWOT is somehow an analysis tool). The rest of this book will take you through the processes you need to really design and implement strategy in your organization. Strategy is not tactics, and while it translates into operational efforts, it is not an operational plan.

It is not easy, but it can be done quickly (if senior management is truly motivated), and it will have a profound impact on your company. I often describe a company that has figured out their strategy and implemented as feeling like the whole organization is running downhill—except with money!

I am both a student and a developer of strategy. I've used this approach for the past twenty-plus years with hundreds of organizations and have taught this approach to tens of thousands as a consultant, an author of five textbooks and many research publications, a professor (*University of Notre Dame, University of Richmond, TCU,* and *Tulane University,* among others), and an internationally known speaker at a wide variety of conferences, trade shows, company retreats, and conventions.

I hope you enjoy this fast-paced look at a complex subject. The concepts are not that difficult to understand. Mastery in application will take time. I have embedded examples while trying not to distract from the message. Therefore, this is a short book (in the world of strategy) meant to be used as a guide to actually getting this done at your company. There are many more nuances to all the approaches discussed in this book; however, they are for the hearty who want to dig deep in the subject.

I encourage you to write me with your feedback, thoughts, stories, and advice. Every company is unique, but the approaches in this book are battle-tested, grounded in good, solid theory, and they employ a very practical version of the latest thinking in the field today. I modified this approach many years ago to account for the realities of business as opposed to the purest, most theoretical take on the subject. By no means will this book answer all your questions, but there is enough here for you to get to work.

Chuck Bamford, Ph.D.
@DrChuckBamford
www.bamfordassociates.com
cbamford@bamfordassociates.com

Charles E. Bamford, Ph.D.

Dr. Chuck Bamford is the managing partner of Charlotte, North Carolina–based Bamford Associates, LLC—a firm focused on the development of implementable strategic plans and an entrepreneurial orientation to growth.

Dr. Bamford worked in M&A/business analysis for twelve years prior to pursuing his Ph.D. A regular speaker at conferences, trade shows, and conventions, he is the author of strategy and entrepreneurship textbooks used by businesses and universities throughout the globe.

His writings include regular contributions to news organizations and the fiction novel, *Some Things Are Never Forgiven*.

A thought leader in the field, his research has been published in the *Strategic Management Journal*, the *Journal of Business Venturing*, *Entrepreneurship Theory and Practice*, the *Journal of Business Research*, the *Journal of Business Strategies*, the *Journal of Managerial Issues*, the *Journal of Technology Transfer*, and the *Journal of Small Business Management*, among others.

Chuck has taught courses in strategy and entrepreneurship at the undergraduate, graduate, and executive levels. He is an adjunct professor of strategy at the *University of Notre Dame* and has taught at universities in Scotland, Hungary, and the Czech Republic. He has been a professor at the *University of Notre Dame, Queens University of Charlotte, University of Richmond, Texas Christian University, and Tulane University*. He has won eighteen teaching excellence awards, including nine Executive

MBA Professor of the Year Awards, and is a Noble Foundation Fellow in Teaching Excellence.

Chuck earned his BS degree at the *University of Virginia* (McIntire School of Commerce), an MBA at *Virginia Tech,* and a Ph.D. in strategy and entrepreneurship at the *University of Tennessee.*

Chapter 1

YOU MUST BE KIDDING!

(Or, We Need to Get Rid of the Myths before We Can Apply Real Strategy)

Before the executives of any organization can get to what constitutes a real strategy (that is, something that actually makes a difference with customers), they have to get their people to abandon the myths. As with most myths, they are grounded in history, are easy to understand, and have some face validity.

If you can't accept that some of these myths exist and might be holding back your organization, then there is no need to read on. Take the blue pill (think *The Matrix*, Morpheus, and a conversation with Neo in the rain), and go back to the world where it will all be OK. I say this only somewhat tongue in cheek. Holding on to myths inhibits your ability to develop real strategy and, more importantly, will virtually prevent you from convincing your employees to take a more profound path.

Letting go of myths can be a painful process—somewhat like an exorcism—but I'll try to give you enough information here to explain why each must be let go. I could write a book on each of these topics with countless examples, but I've tried to keep this concise for your reading and amusement pleasure.

Myth 1: My people are my competitive advantage.

This is the favorite response when I ask executives to describe their strategy or competitive advantage. It is certainly the most politically correct statement that one can make, and if the same executives said that employees are generally interchangeable, they would be accused of... well, everything evil in this world.

The moment that you actually believe that your employees are smarter than your competitors' is the moment that your competitors will start beating you in the market. You have the same (or relatively the same) collection of amazing employees, capable employees, and poor employees as your competitors. All the HR processes in the world today have not changed that dynamic in companies. The employees that you have working in your company are a combination of *luck* (the biggest factor), HR practices, networking, and did I mention *luck*!

"My people are my competitive advantage" (always said with pride).

"Of course they are; none of the competitors have people!"

"Well, our people are better" (now somewhat defensively).

"Sure they are!"

So, here I go. Employees are *not* your competitive advantage—they are how you deliver some of your competitive advantages. I'm not trying to be divisive here, but most of your customers do not generally care (or if they care at all, it is slight) who takes care of their business needs as long as the needs are taken care of. This does not apply to every employee in a company, just most. At every company I have ever worked with or for, there is a contingent of "franchise" employees. Those are employees who, if they left the company, would impact the success of that company quite substantially. We all know who these folks are, and if executives are smart, they take care of these employees to ensure that they stay with the organization. These "franchise" employees are not just the customer-facing employees; they reside throughout an organization.

That said, virtually every other employee is relatively interchangeable. This is because of the customer. The customer is buying from your company for a reason, and in most instances, the employee is simply a conduit for that reason.

- If you walk into the bank to make a deposit, and your favorite teller is not there, you don't walk out in a huff—you make the deposit.
- If you walk into a fast-food restaurant to get a meal, you are indifferent as to who makes the meal or delivers it to you.
- If your power goes out, you don't care who the technician is that turns it back on; you just want the power back on.
- If you call a cruise line to book a trip, you don't really care who is on the other end as long as he or she is competent (friendly is a bonus).
- If you order a new part from a manufacturer, you don't care which employee makes it; you just want the part.
- Do you have any idea who the pilot was on your last flight? No, because it doesn't matter to you as the customer (unless your pilot was Captain Sully Sullenberger, in which case you would have a franchise employee—unfortunately for us, he is retired now). You expect the pilot to be trained, competent, and sober (and personally, I find that a little prayer goes a long way before a flight, but that is a different issue).

This logic can be applied to most employees at most companies in most industries. I've seen it in practice with law firms, where the client may follow the departing attorney or may not; in consulting practices, where the company has a long-term relationship with a firm and is sorry to see that particular consultant, manager, or partner go; in auto dealerships, insurance, manufacturing, banking, and retail stores—you get the picture.

I talked with a bank executive who simply insisted that their competitive advantage was their people. I asked him where they got their people. Of course, they got them from other banks, university recruiting, posts, and luck (much like all their competitors). He insisted that they only hired good employees, and I resisted the desire to ask him if he had ever managed employees that he thought should be fired.

I asked him what he thought the CEO of bank Y (one of his competitors) would say about their own employees.

Might it be something like, "Well, we wish we could say that our employees were our competitive advantage—unfortunately, all the good ones are at X, so all we are left with over here is crap. We just try to do our best with crap employees"?

Of course not! That bank thinks they have the best employees.

This is simply a black hole in strategy. If you are convinced that somehow you have better employees than your competitors, then you distort your business practices to try and take advantage of that aspect.

Customers do not buy from Walmart because they employ Suzie. Despite all the great press about how Costco treats their employees, customers are indifferent as to who checks them out of the store. Customers do not buy a car wash from a particular company because they employ Bill, and they do not deposit their money with Bank of America because they employ Ralph. Customers expect employees to be competent, relatively accommodating, and accountable (as I said earlier, we'll go with friendly as a bonus). We need our employees to do their jobs and do those jobs well, but that is *table stakes* in an industry and is expected out of every competitor. Beyond that, customers are choosing to do business with your company for other reasons. Those reasons will enable you to charge more and may lead to being a company of choice for customers. This is why we have to develop *real* strategy.

Employees are *not* your competitive advantage.

Myth 2: SWOT analysis will allow us to develop a strategy.

SWOT (as applied to the business world) is generally viewed as a creation of the 1970s, when business strategy was really business policy. When I took business policy as an undergraduate student, we read cases to "learn" what to do in business (sadly, some professors still think this is all there is to strategy). Once in business, we were expected to use corporate history or examples in the press as a foundation for what passed as our strategic thinking.

SWOT was an attempt to bring some structure to the topic, and as a conceptual approach, it is still fairly robust. Unfortunately, many authors, academics, and practitioners decided that SWOT was an *analysis* tool and a means for a company to develop its strategy.

SWOT is *not* strategy, and it is *not* an analysis tool. Unless you are simply using it as a team-building exercise, taking five minutes to do a SWOT exercise is a five-minute waste of time at a company. More money has been wasted on SWOT than virtually any other aspect of thought in business. For those of you fortunate enough to not know yet, SWOT is an acronym for **S**trengths, **W**eaknesses, **O**pportunities, and **T**hreats. Anyone can create a SWOT. It is grounded in your own biases and view of the world. In the end, a SWOT is simply the opinion of the person or group filling it out. Companies over the years have dedicated untold dollars to meetings where groups throughout the organization craft the SWOT for their company, their division, their product, etc. Then (of course) you emphasize your strengths, minimize your weaknesses, look for opportunities, and prepare for threats. It all sounds good. However, who decides which element falls into which box?

Just because someone believes X is a strength does not make it so. SWOT is an inherently static look at the business based on a gut opinion. Furthermore, everything that is a strength is also a weakness. By the same token, everything that is an opportunity is also a threat. Occasionally, one element can easily and correctly fit into all four quadrants.

Just for fun, over the years I asked each of my then eight-year-old sons to do a SWOT of his third grade class. I taught each of them the technique in three minutes. The fact that an eight-year-old can learn it effectively in three minutes should tell you everything you need to know about SWOT as tool for crafting million- or billion-dollar decisions.

I then asked his teacher and his principal to each do one. Not surprisingly, none of the three aligned at all. My sons thought that recess and lunch were the strengths of third grade. Each boy also listed his teacher as a strength (albeit below the other two items), a weakness, an opportunity, and a threat (at the top). I know it comes as a shock, but neither the teacher nor the principal listed recess or lunch as strengths. In fact, the teacher and the principal did not agree in any of the four categories.

There are volumes of material out in the Internet world for you to learn about the drawbacks of SWOT as an analysis tool. This approach was abandoned by most serious strategy practitioners more than two decades ago, and yet I see it every year as I work with companies. Its staying power is mostly attributable to its ease of understanding and to the many, many non-strategy professors at universities who "teach" it as a technique.

Serious practitioners of SWOT craft elaborate charts that have a vast list of elements in each of the four boxes. Your view of the company will affect what you believe belongs in each category. However, as I pointed out at the beginning of this piece, SWOT is a fairly robust conceptual approach. If you look at each element, the fact is that you do want to know what would populate each of the four blocks; you just need to use more precise and well-grounded means for getting to each of these.

Do you want to know the strengths of your company? Of course you do. There are well-honed techniques available for getting at the true strengths (differentiators) of your company. It only matters if it helps separate your business from your competitors in the eyes of the customer. Applying these tools will allow you to get a lot closer to a great strategy. Don't let anyone kid you; even with this, strategy is still 50 percent *art*!

Do you want to know the weaknesses of your company? Of course you do. These are the standard elements of the business that are being operated below the median expectations in the industry. It's a weakness if it impacts your customers and prevents them from considering your true strengths. It is crucial to identify these and put together an aggressive action plan to get them at or near the median.

Do you want to know the opportunities of your company? Of course you do. However, it is only an opportunity if you have a competitive advantage that can be applied to it. There are a number of fantastic techniques for crafting these opportunities.

Do you want to know the threats to your company? Of course you do. However, threats affect most of the companies in your industry. Therefore, there are a number of approaches to discern what these might be and how a company can navigate those ahead of its competitors.

What does this mean? It means that it is time to put SWOT to bed as a strategy approach. It is time for every businessperson to learn how to really develop strategy and how it can be implemented.

Don't do SWOT!

Myth 3: The product life cycle will help me decide on a strategy.

The product life cycle (PLC) most certainly exists, and it is quite interesting to view the pattern over time with virtually every product or service. In general, we see a start with some form of introduction followed by a move through growth to maturity, and eventually, it either becomes a commodity (which really means that the rest of the competitors finally caught up, and there is some level of steady sales) or proceeds to some form of slow death. If you follow the logic of the observations, you realize that some products and services stay in a perpetual flatline maturity phase, and others are "reborn," giving the whole product line continued life (think iPhone 15).

It is interesting to note all the effort that is put into trying to figure out where in the life cycle a particular product or service is at a specific time. The theory (according to the marketing folks) is that if you know where you are in the life cycle, then you know how to invest your resources.

All of that would be fine if we had any idea where we were in the life cycle while we were actually in it—which we *do not*. No one can tell you with any precision where computers, cell phones, televisions, or fast-food operations are at the current time. It gets even more muddled when we look at a specific product. Is each slight update to the product a new introduction, and what would that mean for our strategy decisions?

Ask ten people to identify where the Cadillac is on the PLC, and you will get ten locations, each of which is just as reasonable as any of the others. In other words, despite all the statistical efforts to precisely locate the position on the curve, it is simply a guess. Unfortunately, this guess has significant resource implications for the business.

Once a company decides that X product or service is in X stage, it changes the investment approach and expectations. Furthermore, every single product or service has a unique curve (traditionally tied to sales as the vertical axis); therefore, PLC does not even provide an insight as to the level of investment or expectations that should be planned.

You know where you are in the life cycle only long after the product or service has ceased to be of practical value. PLC works very well as a historical observation and is simply useless as a tool for understanding current or future strategic approaches.

Strategy is about making decisions that will impact the company in the future. Those decisions must be made in the present, with information that is of value in the present. We simply do not know where we are in the PLC until long after it has happened; therefore, it is *not* a technique that assists the design of strategy.

Strategists don't waste time on PLC!

Myth 4: We shouldn't look at what competitors are doing— let's focus on what we do.

Here's one that somehow made it into the lore of exceptional business leadership. If you follow some of the interviews that have been broadcast over the years, you will find some leaders who insist that they pay no attention to competitors, as though that somehow made their successes more impressive.

It is hard to find a way to support this approach even on its face when we know that customers compare any product or service we offer to other alternatives. While we may have a core group of dedicated, loyal customers who will never consider the competition, this group of "perfect customers" is rarely big enough to allow a business to grow.

Customers compare every offering, every product, and every aspect of a business not only to your direct competitors but also to other means of achieving a similar result. An individual customer who has a headlight out on his or her car has a lot of possible solutions available that will involve purchasing a bulb. He or she can buy a bulb at any of the national auto parts chains (Advanced Auto, AutoZone, Napa, Pep Boys, etc.) if planning to change it himself or herself. The same individual could go to any national chain or local mechanic to have it done, or go to the dealership, or simply not change the thing. All of these are options to the customer, and each one gets weighed based on the customer's own rational approach.

When the offering by the competition exceeds some internal threshold with the customer, that person is no longer our customer. I am continuously struck by the lack of knowledge (from the perspective of the consumer) of the competitors and their offerings. Assumptions are made that have a dramatic impact on the positioning of products and services.

We simply *must* know what our competitors are doing, how they are doing it, and how that might impact our sales. A deep understanding of the competitors is the first step in designing a strategy. Trying to craft a strategy in isolation may feel comforting at the time, but you do a huge disservice to your company when you don't run the company from the perspective that your customers use to make decisions.

Know your competitors!

Myth 5: Quality or customer service is our strategic advantage.

Customers certainly care about quality. That is to say, customers expect to receive slightly better quality than they paid for. Most customers assume quality to the point that the product or service performs as or slightly better than expected. Most customers have no idea what constitutes "quality" or how to evaluate it. It is a mantra in business that quality is the cornerstone of customer choice. It is not always or even generally true. By the way, customers (B2B or B2C)[1] will certainly tell you that quality is an issue in their purchases; it is just not why they are buying.

When you put your strategy stake in the ground and claim that you are the quality choice for customers, you have put yourself in the position of proving it to customers in terms that customers care about and can actually see for themselves. In general, this means that you have to be so far above the rest of the industry that it is obvious to customers. Anything short of this and the competitors can easily negate your so-called competitive advantage. Be very wary of this seductive approach.

It is shocking how many companies seem to truly believe that their strategy revolves around customer service. It is what differentiates us in the market! The drumbeat of customer service as our strategic differentiator is used by virtually everyone. While it is certainly politically correct, this one is so far from being true that it is laughable.

Now let's be clear—it would be wonderful if customer service were really the cornerstone of a business. The entire business would be focused on the needs of the customer, and each customer would feel that he or she was truly important to the company. The customer would bypass your competitors in order to enjoy the feeling that he or she had when doing business with your company.

---

1 Business to Business (B2B) and Business to Consumer (B2C)

When was the last time you felt that way at your bank, gas station, cleaner's, utility, fast-food restaurant, lawyer, doctor, university, or other organization? The answer is not much and not consistently.

A basic tenet of strategy is that whatever constitutes the elements of your competitive advantages must be consistently seen by the customer. Instead, despite all the investment, talk, and management firepower aimed at improving customer service, the reality on the ground is as follows:

- **"We can't refund your money."**
  - o Are you kidding me? Give your money back to you?
- **"Our systems don't allow us to do that."**
  - o They were designed in a patchwork system by IT folks who don't deal with customers.
- **"You needed to show us that first."**
  - o Prove it.
- **"I know we said that, but…"**
  - o Hey, sometimes we'll say anything to get you to buy.
- **"That is the way we handle all customers; you are not being treated unfairly."**
  - o Sucky is as sucky does, and we do sucky really well.
- **"I wish we could do that, but…"**
  - o It is not my fault that we won't accommodate you.
- **"Could I put you on hold?"**
  - o Not really a question. This really means I'll get back to you when I'm ready.
- **"Would you read me the error code on your screen?"**
  - o We expect the customer to be our quality control.
- **"The manager should be back shortly."**
  - o You are clearly asking for special treatment, and that will cost you!

I'm sure you can add many more quotes to the refrain of "the customer is *not* the most important element in our business" mantra and therefore not one of our competitive differentiators.

For the *vast* majority of companies, customer service is just table stakes. It is one of those areas where the company needs to be within a reasonable distance of the average for the industry (actually measured as the median by strategists). Some industries have a very high median level of expected customer service, while others are simply abysmal.

A lot of money spent beefing up what passes for customer service is only of value if the company can achieve a level of service that is so far above the competitors that customers truly notice the difference. Otherwise, it is a waste of time, money, and resources to do much more than what is expected in your industry. In other words, customer service is only rarely a strategy; mostly it consists of empty words into which companies pour money.

Be very wary of quality or customer service as a strategy!

Myth 6: Low cost is the key to our strategy.

Virtually every company at some point in its existence has had an executive convince the senior leadership team that cost cutting is a strategy. Top lines are not growing as hoped, competition is getting tougher, and bonuses are being cut. Executives are convinced that the company can attain a competitive advantage by making Herculean efforts to lower costs (or at least earn their bonuses in the short run—probably the real reason).

Interestingly enough, this is absolutely true—for *one* company in your competitive set. While cost containment is generally advisable as a tactic (as long as it does not impact the strategy being pursued by the company), only one company in any particular industry can actually be the low-cost leader. Everyone else is simply a wannabe without the ability to attain the same basis-point margins as the low-cost leader. The true low-cost leader can lower prices to the point where competitors are simply not profitable (think the PC industry) while still maintaining healthy margins.

This means that the time, effort, resources, and mental firepower that are spent trying to continuously drive costs from the business will only help the bottom line if the following occur:

1) Your business is truly the low-cost leader,
2) You are driving out costs from areas that customers do not use to make a "buy" decision (the orthodox parts of the organization), or
3) You have compelling competitive advantages (the *strategy* of the company) beyond price, and you *protect* those areas from the cost cutting.

You generally can't cut your way to success.

15

Cost cutting is a tactic that should appropriately be applied to any element of the business that is considered table stakes in the industry. You should apply all the well-known techniques for efficiency to those areas of the business that are not true competitive advantages of the organization.

Other than that, remember that customers couldn't care less whether you are the low-cost leader. No customer buys from you because you need them to buy from you. No customer cares about whether you are earning a fair return on whatever you are selling; they simply evaluate the perceived value they are receiving for the amount of money they are spending.

There is a big difference between low cost and low price. In every industry and in every product or service offering, there are a group of customers that will only buy from you if you are the low-price leader. Chasing these customers is intelligent *only* if you are the low-cost leader.

Anyone can be the low-price leader as long as they are willing to sacrifice margins. Competing to be the low-price alternative is a strategic spiral to mediocrity at best and bankruptcy at worst, unless you really are the low-cost leader at the same time.

So, low cost can indeed be a strategy—for *one* organization in each industry. It can be incredibly effective for that one company, but it is only for one company. Every other company in an industry needs a real strategy (a set of true competitive advantages) that will be the focus of everyone in the company.

There is only one low-cost competitor!

Myth 7: Our brand is our strategy.

Brands are incredibly powerful symbols for both employees and customers. A well-crafted brand image can certainly draw in customers while allowing the company to charge a premium price. However, a brand is *not* a strategy. It is what makes up (creates) that brand that is the strategy. Every company has a brand, and we have seen brands come and go over the years. A brand like Sony was the pinnacle of technological innovation and cachet in the 1990s at a time when Apple was considered a niche player in the computer field. The names have not changed significantly (albeit Apple moved away from Apple Computer), and yet the "brand" is completely different. Sears was the go-to store for decades and is now fighting for survival. This ebb and flow of brands happens all the time.

It is important to understand that a brand has no value without a strong set of competitive advantages supporting it. As companies fail to continuously design and effectively implement real strategies, the brand loses value. Fortunately, for most brands, this decline is gradual, as customers have institutional memory. This provides a continuous window within which company executives can develop real strategies that truly separate the company from its competitors and then tie those elements to the brand.

Brand is *not* a competitive advantage.

Chapter 2

A STRATEGY MODEL THAT WORKS

Strategy is iterative, sequential, and continuous. There is a path to follow if you want to develop a solid strategy for your company that separates it from its competitors. In this chapter I outline the approach and the fundamentals of the model. The chapters that follow will examine each element of this overall model.

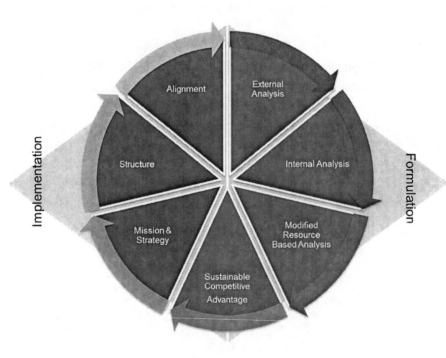

Good strategy design starts external to the organization. There is simply no way to develop a strategy without putting yourself in the shoes of the customer and viewing the choices for your product or service the way that customers see those choices.

Strategy starts with a deep understanding of the competition and the customers. Customers are constantly comparing your offerings with those of your competitors. From a strategy perspective, there are four key areas that need to be understood, all of which will be discussed in detail in chapter 3.

First, every product or service offering has a perfect customer. That is a customer that instantly gets the value proposition and is willing to pay you for it. Second, a comparison competitive set must be established in order to evaluate your offerings relative to those of your direct competitors. We will discuss the use of "bump" competitors, median expectations, and metrics. Third, it is necessary to evaluate the offerings of your organization from the perspective of both real and perceived switching costs. Finally, we need to map the touch points with the customer. Every touch point with the customer is an opportunity to press home the competitive advantages of the company.

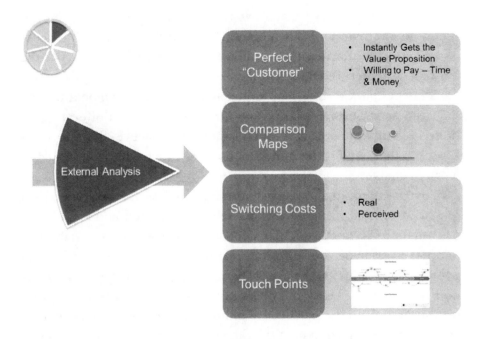

Once there is a solid foundation of external analysis in place, we can turn our attention inside the organization. The first step in that process is to define what parts of the organization are standard (ordinary, typical, orthodox, expected, or whatever term you prefer) and what parts of the organization are potentially exceptional (extraordinary, remarkable, unorthodox, differentiating, or whatever term you prefer). There are many elements of any organization that must be in place for the business to be considered a player in the market. In fact, most of what is done at most organizations most days is the standard (orthodox) operations that must be done by virtually every business in the industry. We will discuss all this at length in chapter 4.

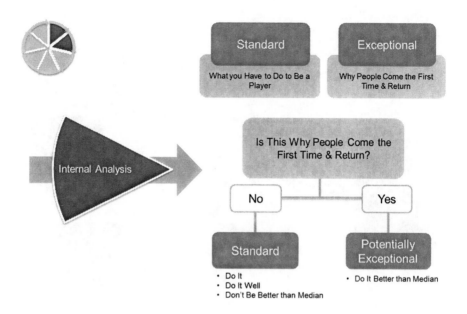

Knowing the elements of the organization that are standard allows us to establish those areas where resource investments can be restricted (as long as these are at or near the median for the industry) in order to channel those resources into something that truly makes a difference with the customer. Those elements (resources or capabilities) that the business team believes have the potential to be separators—that is, potentially exceptional—can now be evaluated to see if they are truly competitive advantages for the organization. This is best done with a modified application of resource-based analysis (RBA).

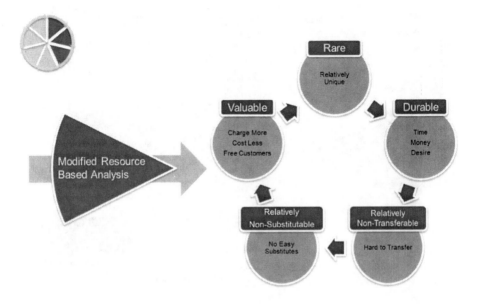

RBA (or variations on the same approach) is the predominant approach to strategy available today. It is (and has been for some time) the state of the art in strategic thinking for both academics and practitioners. Most practicing strategists modified the approach long ago to make it more applicable to businesses. We will discuss this approach in detail in chapter 5.

Once we have developed a short list of those elements that are true resource-based advantages—that is, those resources and capabilities that pass all five elements of RBA—we have the set of elements that constitute the organization's true competitive advantages at this point in the life of the business. The same approach will be used to evaluate new potential competitive advantages in order to incorporate those into the business.

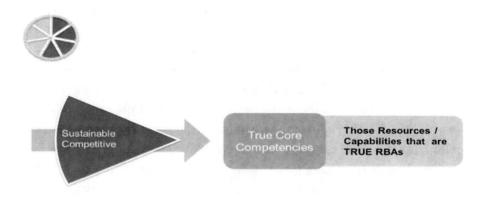

From this point forward in the analysis, the effort turns from strategy formulation to strategy implementation. Once the organization has a solid handle on what truly separates it from the competitors in the eyes of the customer, it is necessary to get the entire organization focused around those elements.

A great strategy must be driven down through the organization in such a manner that every single employee in the organization knows precisely why the customer truly pays the company. No matter what the marketing hype says, customers don't really buy a Rolex watch for its precision (precision helps, but status is more important), a Cadillac SUV Hybrid for its fuel efficiency (there are far cheaper vehicles with better performance), Beats headsets for their low profile (seeing every major athlete wear a set has a lot to do with sales), McDonald's salads for their health benefits (it's a compromise so that the kids can eat what they want to eat), or tickets to fly the friendly skies of United

(In 2014 ACSI ranked United Airlines dead last in customer service).[2] A focus on these types of elements, while probably well intentioned, is a waste of resources on things that are standard.

The areas to focus on in implementation are (1) the mission of the organization, (2) the metrics that will be used to measure strategic success, and (3) the alignment of the message with employees. Although many organizations claim to have a mission statement (or claim that there is no value in having a mission statement), the fact remains that it can be a powerful, unifying symbol for employees and customers alike. Tied tightly to the competitive advantages of the business, it allows everyone in the organization to have a common purpose. That, in combination with metrics (gates in some instances) that are tied to the strategy of the business,

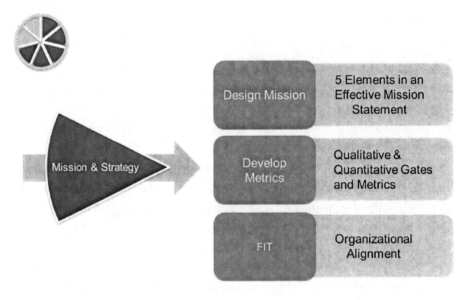

---

2 G. Karp, "Airline Customer Rankings Fall on Service, Uncomfortable Seats," Chicago Tribune, April 21, 2014, http://articles.chicagotribune.com/2014-04-21/business/chi-airline-customer-satisfaction-rankings-20140421_1_northwest-airlines-continental-airlines-american-airlines.

gives everyone a means of measuring success. Strategy metrics are not traditional financial measures, customer counts, or satisfaction surveys. They are means of measuring activity related to the strategy of the business.

All businesses measure outcomes; this is a means of measuring inputs. The delay between inputs and outcomes with strategy measures can be significant, and yet it is crucial for senior management and the board of directors to truly *know* that their strategies are being implemented. Finally, all of this must be communicated to the organization in a succinct, continuous, and consistent manner for everyone to get the message and apply it to their jobs. All of this will be examined at some length in chapter 6.

Structure follows strategy. This is a fundamental rule in strategy that is lost in many businesses. The next step is to use the structure of the organization to get the strategy implemented.

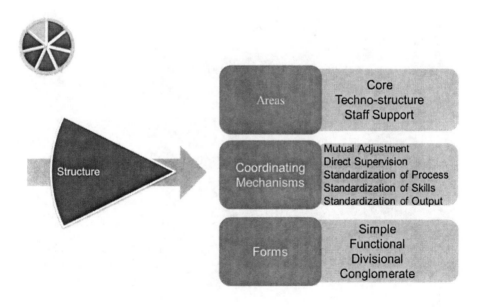

Unlike most books on the subject that start with the type of structure (functional, divisional, etc.), we take a well-developed approach that was originally crafted by Henry Mintzberg in the late 1970s. Research and practical appplication has modified this approach so that it can be utilized by any organization, and ties the structure directly to the strategy. That process has three elements to it. The first is to divide up the organization based on each area's impact on the competitive advantages of the business. The second is to figure out the best method of coordinating the work within each of those areas. The final element is to combine that into a structure that is both efficient and easily understood. Far too much time is wasted by employees trying to figure out whom to work with in order to get something done. This complex and critical subject will be covered in chapter 7.

The final piece of the pie is the alignment of all the aforementioned elements. We generally break this up into four distinct efforts, with the last being the most powerful tool we have found in implementation.

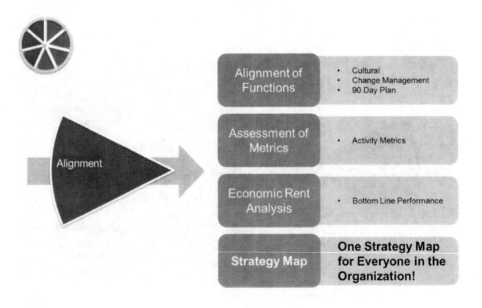

All the functions in the organization must put together a detailed project plan that incorporates the strategy elements that will be needed and the cultural realities that must be dealt with in order to move the organization down its new path. The metrics laid out earlier in the process are benchmarked and tracked. The overall impact on the organization's financials are calculated, approved, and tracked. This leads to the development of the *strategy map.*

Every single employee in the organization will have a single-page strategy map. That map is grounded in the competitive advantages of the business and personalized for every employee.

Strategy Map

Perfect Customer:
Comparison Set:

Standard Operations: What we must do to be a player in the industry

Value Driver	Stakeholder Statements	Need From the Company	Must Do Individually	Metrics
		What do WE need from the organization to make this happen?	*What must I do to make this happen?*	

NOTE: Red font question will be filled out by each individual in the organization.

The first, second, third, and last columns are consistent throughout the organization, while the individual employee fills out the fourth column. This column requires each employee to detail out what he or she can do to make the strategy a reality. A critical performance element of strategy implementation is the ability of every employee to have an impact on those strategies. The second column is where the organization converts the competitive advantages of the business into statements that they would want to hear customers make about the business relative to that particular competitive advantage. This mapping technique, approach, and implementation will be discussed in chapter 8.

This model constitutes *strategy*!

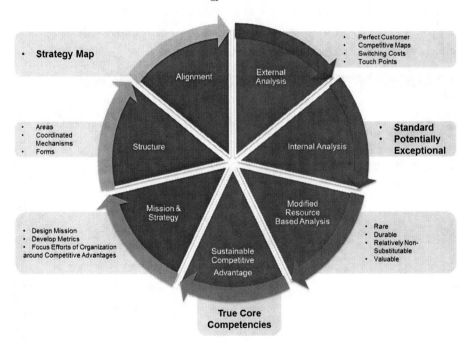

Chapter 3

KNOW YOUR CUSTOMERS AND YOUR COMPETITORS

The path to a great strategy starts by looking outside the organization. There are many, many ways for organizations to dedicate enormous resources to understanding the market. Whole departments have been created to generate information and provide so-called competitive intelligence. One look at any strategy textbook or a short conversation with one of the big consulting companies and you will realize that there are dozens of techniques available. My recommendations are relatively simple, extraordinarily easy to explain to employees, and they provide sufficient insight into the competitive market for an organization to position itself to craft a strategy. In this case, sufficient is not a bad word. No amount of data analysis will provide you with insurance against bad judgment.

Generally, I prefer not to overkill the analysis. Use what you want or are comfortable with, but ensure that you have a good grasp on your customer's perspective of the market. Here are the four key means that executives can use to gain a strategic grasp on the environment.

1) Deep understanding of the *perfect customer*
2) A narrow comparison set of competitors along with a series of two-dimensional maps
3) An understanding of the real and perceived switching costs from the customer's perspective

4) A map of the points where your business touches the customer, ensuring that every touch point reinforces the strategy of the business

Perfect Customer

Every business that has sales has a perfect customer. A perfect customer (by definition) is one that

a) Instantly understands your value proposition, and
b) Is willing to pay you for it.

I like to think of the perfect customer as a circle in the middle of a bull's-eye.

Every business that you have ever worked for, every business on the Fortune 500, and every business that you can think of started as an entrepreneurial venture that was created by one person or a small group of people. Over time, because they had a value proposition and a set of customers that paid for that value proposition, they were able to grow the business.

At some point, virtually all businesses hit the wall with the number of perfect customers who are going to buy from them. In order to grow, they are forced to draw in customers that don't instantly get the value proposition and may not willing to pay the same price for it that your perfect customers are willing to pay.

The perfect customer for an airport coffee shop might be the one who has to take an early flight and cannot imagine functioning in the morning without a cup of coffee. He or she has passed through security and is staring at the only coffee shop in the terminal. What could that coffee shop *really* charge for a cup of coffee sold to that person? It is midnight, and your flight has been cancelled. You need a rental car to get to your destination (only a two-hour drive away—something that has happened to me). Perfect customer! Or ponder the folks who used to stand in line at midnight to get the latest iPhone. What could you charge these perfect customers? They instantly get the value proposition. The more compelling this value proposition is, the stronger your position to charge.

As the business grows, it makes decisions that have the potential to impact its perfect customers, destroy its strategy, impact its net cash flow, and yet appear to be successful for a while because sales go up.

If we could run a successful business that never had to move past the group that constitutes our perfect customers, we could constantly refine the offering and enjoy a business that perfectly matched our capabilities with the needs of our customers. Unfortunately, in order to grow, most businesses must try to reach out and satisfy more and more customers. This is where companies develop problems. In order to attract these new (and significantly larger) customer groups, the company resorts to a variety of strategy-destroying techniques such as

1) Price reductions
2) Sale pricing
3) Discounting
4) Special deals
5) Cost savings measures that impact the customer experience
6) Introduction of more and more new products or services that distract from the original value proposition and cause logistics and procedural nightmares
7) Outsourcing elements of the business that impact the customer experience

It is unfortunate for the long-term strategy that as the company begins making these strategy-destroying moves, top-line sales increase or costs drop, and often, they do so quickly. Think about how Cross Pens moved from being a special gift to being available at every drugstore, or how US Airways outsourced elite traveler customer service until repeated complaints from their coveted business travelers finally forced a move back to Winston-Salem, North Carolina.

There comes a point in all these moves where the company goes too far and loses the core (perfect) customer that it once had. In some cases this spells the demise of the organization. In other cases the moves have been so dramatic that a new perfect customer has been formed, and the business continues. General Electric has ebbed and flowed over the years such that today it looks nothing like it did in 1980. In the process, they isolated, packaged, and sold business units that had fallen from their famed number-one or number-two market share position. Those businesses were sold to organizations that thrived on that unit's particular perfect customer. Strategy is about returns!

The key to this understanding of your perfect customer is the guidance that it provides to management. We want strategic moves that are purposeful, consistent, long lasting, and considered. A deep understanding of the perfect customer is core to the company's ability to craft a strategy and design an organization around that strategy. We expect senior management to try and grow the company. It is the focus on the perfect customer that can provide the compass—but not a precise compass, as strategy is about nuance. I like to remind everyone that strategy is an "ish" approach. General direction will put your organization far ahead of your competitors.

How far can the senior leadership team push their organization past the perfect customer group, and can they pull it back when they go too far? Starbucks has been one of the greatest, most recent examples of this push and pull. Howard Schultz has proven his ability to master the focus on the perfect customer, flow the business out from that perfect customer, and pull it back when the business has strayed too far.

Starbucks's backstory is well-known, and the fact that Starbucks coffeehouses are ubiquitous is a testament to their understanding of the customer. The company ventured from a classic coffeehouse (including selling mugs, etc.) to a seller of music, film, and books. The company has experimented with beer service after 4:00 p.m. in some locations and bought out tea purveyor Teavana. After rebranding the company from Starbucks Coffee to Starbucks in early 2011, the company has moved strongly into the grocery aisles, with a variety of products well beyond coffee.

After stepping back from day-to-day management, Schultz returned to run the company in 2008. The company had faltered in almost every way possible. Howard Schultz wrote an open letter to the entire organization about commoditization and the need to return Starbucks to a unique position in the market. He noted that many of the decisions made during the previous few years had been well-meaning and even data driven, but that the sum of the decisions resulted in the loss of the value proposition for the perfect customer. They had moved to automated machines that were so tall that you couldn't talk to the barista making your coffee. They produced vacuum-packed coffee, whose unintended consequence was that the customers couldn't enjoy the smell of ground coffee in the stores anymore. They used cookie-cutter store designs that felt institutional instead of the intended third place that Schultz had cultivated for decades. Starbucks had also started providing hot lunch sandwiches, which put smells into the air (think burned cheese) that had customers mentally comparing the business with fast-food restaurants.

He told the employees in his open letter (available on the web), "I have said for twenty years that our success is not an entitlement, and now it's proving to be a reality. Let's be smarter about how we are spending our time, money, and resources. Let's get back to the core. Push for innovation, and do the things necessary to once again differentiate Starbucks from all others."

Why does the perfect customer want to pay four dollars or more for a cup of coffee? Is it about being seen with the Starbucks cup? Is it about being able to get exactly what the customers want? Is it about the baristas knowing their names and their favorite drinks? Is it about having a unique language that makes you feel a part of a closed society (think grande, venti, trenta). It is something well beyond the drink, and for the perfect customer, the value proposition is compelling enough to pay a *vast* premium for the cup.

This understanding of the perfect customer group can be developed in many ways, but in an existing business, one of the best (and easiest) is to examine which customers consistently use your products or services and don't complain about the price! Ever watch people line up at an Apple store the day before a new product release? Wait in long lines to attend a movie? Put up with less-than-ideal conditions to buy something on Black Friday (or Thursday as the case may now be)? You get the picture. There are dozens (if not hundreds) of techniques that can be used. I have my own favorites. Use what works for you and your organization, but make sure you have put yourself in your customer's position.

Know who your perfect customer is, and be able to describe why they are buying from you.

Comparison Competitive Set

Once you have a handle on the perfect customer, you can develop the comparison competitive set. It is important to understand that this is not every competitor that exists in your industry. Instead, it is that group of competitors that your perfect customer is using when he or she considers buying from your organization. We generally refer to this group as our "bump" competitors. Bump competitors are those competitors that you most often lose sales to and those who most often lose sales to you. If your perfect customer did not buy from you, whom did he or she buy from? If that perfect customer chose you, whom did he or she not choose in this particular instance? Why that customer bought is a whole different discussion.

In order to develop an effective strategy, it is necessary to have a comparison competitive set. Strategy is relative, not absolute. Your customers do not view the product or service offerings of your business in isolation from your competitors, and in that same vein, neither should you.

The list of competitors must be actual companies, not generic groups of companies. Customers evaluate your product or service offering against other real companies, not concepts. In the best of circumstances, we strongly recommend that an organization (or a part of an organization, if the perfect customer changes from area to area in the organization) have no more than five competitors in the comparison set. Once the analysis gets above five, it becomes increasingly more difficult to evaluate the strategy. Interestingly, most research suggests that customers narrow their comparisons down to just a few competitors when making a "buy" decision. This is true with both retail and commercial "buy" decisions.

Whom does Starbucks really compete with? It depends on which part of the business we are considering. Let's take the coffeehouse business and presume for a moment (this is simply my outside view as an example) that their perfect customer stops by every morning on the way to work and orders a specialty drink (and generally the same one every day)—you know the ones—iced venti, decaf, thirteen-pump caramel, whole-milk latte. The only place that order would be understood is at Starbucks. The customer uses his or her gold loyalty card and could make the drink at home, but it takes time, lots of products and a delicate machine. The customer prefers to grab a pastry (a decadent little treat that adds hundreds of calories to his or her day, but something the customer wouldn't even consider having in the house) with the drink. Look at the businesses that could be (and I emphasize "could be," as I do not have access to their data) in their comparison competitive set:

1) **McDonald's**—Serves coffee and some specialty drinks, but it is hit-or-miss as to whether they will be able to make exactly what you want (they keep tweaking their offering). They don't really have pastries, although they do have lots of food choices. They don't have a loyalty card at the time of this writing (amazingly), and the feel of the place is quite different. *Probably not a good candidate for the competitor list.*

35

2) **Panera**—They are able to handle the specialty drinks and have a good selection (probably a bigger one) of pastries. They have a loyalty card and an easy feel that probably matches up well with Starbucks (usually a bigger area with more seating choices). *Good addition to the competitor list.*

3) **Duncan Donuts**—Generally basic coffee products (although they are also trying to expand their offering). No pastries, but a wide selection of donuts (equally decadent) and bagels. They have a loyalty card. The atmosphere is more austere and less welcoming to customers wanting to stay for a bit. *Probably not a good candidate for the competitor list.*

4) **Caribou**—Capable of making any type of specialty coffee or tea product that Starbucks can make. Equivalent pastry and food operation. Good atmosphere that competes well. Only open in eight states after the 2012 buyout by German company Joh. A. Benckiser. *Probably a good candidate for the competitor list.*

The list could go on to include some local coffeehouses or more international chains such as Tim Horton's or Caffè Ritazza that do a particularly good job, or you could include some of the companies that I ruled out. Despite what some might tell you, there is no scientific means for deciding who should be on this list. Keep the focus on the perfect customer, use available data, draw inferences, be a student of your competitors, and establish your comparison competitive set.

Once this is complete, the company needs to compare where they stand relative to that set of competitors. At this point in the analysis, I suggest that the company use standard, easily collected metrics or metrics of particular interest to the company at the time. Once the company has figured out what their true competitive advantages are, they will be in a position to establish metrics that are more precisely aligned with the strategy. At this point, we are just trying to set a beginning point for discussion.

A series of two-dimensional charts can be used to graphically show relative position on each metric chosen. The horizontal axis lists your company and those in your comparison competitive set, while the vertical axis represents the metric being used (whether it is quantitative or qualitative). Keep the horizontal axis consistent, and the executives in the organization will have a set of charts that not only show where the organization exists in the present time, but also can be used to track changes over time.

Real and Perceived Switching Costs

Every customer has his or her own set of switching costs while evaluating one competitor's offerings versus another competitor's offerings. There are real switching costs—those that require the customer to spend money in order to switch from your product or service to a competitor's or that require the investment of significant time (usually learning or setup) in order to switch. There are also perceived switching costs that, while relatively intangible, are nonetheless quite powerful. Perceived switching costs do not involve the expenditure of extra time or financial resources on the part of the customer, but they may be powerfully ingrained in the mind of the customer.

Real switching costs constitute a powerful set of real barriers for established organizations. Once the customer of a bank has started a checking account, opened a savings account, established a safe-deposit box, and most importantly, taken the time to insert every one of his or her bills into the online bill pay system, the real costs for that customer to switch banks is significant. It is a time-consuming effort and therefore one that provides real switching costs.

The imbuing of real switching costs is a powerful barrier to new entrants and provides a means for organizations to charge more or ensure continued business (within reason). At some point, the bank could frustrate the customer (raise prices too high, treat the customer very poorly, fall behind in technology, etc.) to such a point that the customer is willing to incur the switching costs. By the same token, a competitor could expend the time, effort, or resources to reduce the switching costs to zero (or below) in order to encourage switching.

Prior to the big recession that started in 2008, Bank of America instituted an interesting program aimed at attacking real switching costs. They offered to pay new customers to open an account. Customers could open the account online and receive seventy-five dollars. The bet was that people would view the money as ample pay for the effort to open an account at BofA (reducing the real switching costs). Having paid the customer seventy-five dollars, BofA hoped that customers would discover for themselves how technologically adept the bank really was and would move their account activity over to BofA. If you could accurately assess the amount of effort this would require and then calculate the value of your time, you could assess whether BofA had reduced your real switching costs to zero (or below, in some cases).

Real switching costs come in many forms—loyalty cards for discounts (grocery stores), mileage programs (airlines), points programs (hotels), volume discounts (B2B), familiarity in function (cell phones), and speed of payment (billing), to name a few. Perceived switching costs are those costs that are far more intangible, but in many cases more powerful. These costs are those felt by the customer about the product, service, or company. There are no real switching costs associated with moving from Coke to Pepsi or vice versa. Both are quite easy to find and have virtually the same pricing, the bottles and cans open with the same ease, and you don't have to learn how to swallow all over again. Fundamentally, they are both caramel-colored, sweetened, carbonated water. Yet, try to get a die-hard Coca-Cola drinker to switch to Pepsi. They simply cannot imagine holding the blue can or drinking it. Coke is Mom, America, and apple pie, while Pepsi is the new generation and hip. They have imbued these characteristics into the very essence of what it means to drink one or the other.

Consider what a Coca-Cola commercial at Christmas looks like. It is cute little polar bears sliding down a snowbank into a group of penguins and *not* eating the penguins. Amazingly, they all enjoy a Coke together. Can you just hear the following:

> I'd like to teach the world to sing
> In perfect harmony.
> I'd like to buy the world a Coke
> And keep it company.

OK, maybe not, but the essence is there. Pepsi is rock concerts, active people, and more importantly, the latest hip people. Over time, they have used Joanie Sommers, Michael Jackson, Ray Charles, Britney Spears, Christina Aguilera, and Beyoncé, to name but a few. Whoever is hot has a shot at being the latest Pepsi idol.

These companies don't talk about the cleanliness of their commercial vats. They don't talk about the logistics systems, the bottling operations, the cool new features, and so on. Soda (and especially caramel-colored sugar water) has virtually no real switching costs. Just look at how many companies have tried to produce and sell the same stuff under their brand name (think Sam's Choice, RC Cola, Nehi, Double Cola, Jolt Cola, Schweppes Cola, and Like Cola, and you get the picture).

Perceived switching costs permeate the entire landscape of competitive choice. We have views about automobiles that generally have little to do with the data, as well as opinions about clothing brands, computer brands, restaurants, suppliers, shipping companies, and so on.

Perceived switching costs can be powerful, but they are also highly vulnerable. Since the customer can really switch quite easily, it is important to maintain the image rigorously and consistently throughout the entire organization. If we are the "fun ships" (Carnival), then we have to ensure that every employee understands what that means and is unflinching in its application. These perceived switching costs are glass houses for organizations, and they require extraordinary attention to detail.

It is ideal to have a nice mix of switching costs in the products, services, or organization. Carefully developed, they provide the backdrop for our pivot to examine the company from the inside.

Touch Points

The final piece to the external examination (the foundation of good strategy) is the mapping of the touch points with the customer. Managing the touch points—those times when your company has direct contact with the customer in any way—is an important part of understanding and later implementing the strategy.

A consistent element of strategy effectiveness has been the concept of *fit* and *alignment.* Customers judge a company based on whether they can rely on a consistent experience. Any time that experience varies (for whatever reason), the clarity of the strategy gets confused for the customer. Unfortunately, confusing the strategy opens the door for the customer to consider other competitors.

Consider the way that you are treated at your favorite restaurant. Nine straight times you are approached for your drink choice within a minute of sitting down. The wait staff are attentive to your needs, and the food quality and portions are consistent. Then, on your tenth visit, everything is different. You wait much longer to be asked about drinks, you feel as though you are begging to get service, and the portion sizes of your meal are smaller. You make the decision to come again despite your misgivings, and the experience changes once again, with portion sizes back to normal but a long wait to get greeted the first time.

The lack of consistency (in this case a very simple example) frustrates most customers and causes them to look around for alternatives. I've seen the exact same type of inconsistent experience muddy the compelling strategies in the relationships with manufacturing suppliers, law firms, lawn care professionals, hotel chains, Internet providers, contractors of every type—you get the picture.

In order to really ensure that, regardless of what is happening within the company, the customer has a consistent experience, it is necessary (or at least advisable) to map the touch points with the customer. Each customer interaction with any type of company should be tracked, scripted so that the experience is consistent, and aligned with the strategy goals of the company. Do not miss a chance to bring home the reason that your organization has been chosen by the customer—hopefully one or more of your competitive advantages—with each and every interaction.

Mapping should be done graphically as well as in a spreadsheet (or project management-type tracking form) with the conditions as they exist right now that outlines the following:

1) Every contact between a company and its customers
2) The purpose of the contact from the customer's perspective
3) The strategy point(s) that the company currently "messages" during the contact
4) The current result of the contact with the customer

It is an important baseline piece of information for the establishment of strategy, and once a solid strategy is in place, it is an important piece of the implementation of that strategy. After the strategy has been developed, the elements that need to be tracked include the following:

1) Every contact between a company and its customers
2) The purpose of the contact from the customer's perspective
3) The strategy point(s) that the company wants to "message" during the contact
4) The desired result of the contact with the customer

Chapter 4

STANDARD STUFF AND MAYBE SOME EXCEPTIONAL STUFF

Armed with a solid understanding of the market in which the business competes, we now turn our attention inward and examine the business.

One of the mistakes made by many, many managers, leaders, business owners, and executives (whatever title encourages you pay attention) is the view that everything in the company has to excel. I had the following conversation with the CEO of a Fortune 200 company.

CEO: "Look, Chuck, I've spent my entire life managing big corporations, and I view a business as a *boat* [said with a lot of emphasis]. I want everything in the company to be the very best. I want the best manufacturing, the best sales force, the best payroll department, and the best administrative assistants in world. I push everyone to excel; I invest heavily in every area of the business so that as a whole we are the very best. It's like a boat. When you push everyone to the highest level and invest in every aspect of the business, then the whole boat rises."

Me: "Wow. It would probably be a useful analogy for the organization if it was a *boat* [said with an equal amount of emphasis]. But it is not a boat. It is a company that customers buy things from, and no customer has ever come in the front door and said, 'Well, I just want you to know that I've heard you have a first-class payroll department, and because of that, I bypassed all your competitors to buy from you.' Customers don't care about your payroll department, your janitorial service, how nice the chairs are that employees sit in, or how sophisti-

42

cated your back-office IT works. These items are standard. That is, they are the things you do and have to have in order to be considered by a customer. Standard elements of the business are not why customers choose one business over another, but they are the important table stakes to be in the game."

Virtually every business (OK, every business) can be separated into those areas that are standard and those areas that are potentially exceptional (we'll get to that in a minute). Most of what is done, most days, by most employees is standard operations.

- The standard elements of any business must be done. If you fail to meet the standard requirements (for your business) of your customers, then they will stop buying from your organization.
- The standard elements of any business must be done well.
- However, the standard elements of any business need only be done at the median expectation level within the comparison competitive set.

What constitutes standard is decided upon by the customer and only by the customer. Furthermore, the level of the bar is always moving up. What was once special, unique, rare, or unorthodox becomes standard over time. Our expectations as customers are constantly moving up.

Companies that started up their web pages in the 1990s were cutting edge. Today, we not only expect to find everything on the web; we also expect to transact much of our business that way. A cell phone in the 1990s was able to make a phone call (most of the time). Today, we barely care if we can make phone calls. Most of the wireless companies have moved to unlimited calls, because the name of the game is data. Not that long ago, college applications were tedious affairs involving a lot of paper and overnight delivery. Today, the whole process is done electronically, much to the dismay of FedEx, UPS, and other carriers. The list goes on and on, with obvious ramifications.

Meeting the median expectations for the standard elements of the business is crucial to the success of the business. Imagine being at a high-end restaurant and having dirty silverware at your table. You send it back, and what comes back is more dirty silverware with old food encrusted on it! We have an expectation that the silverware will be clean. We don't really know what clean is (the presumption is that if we don't see anything on it, then it must be clean), but we want to believe it is clean.

The restaurant could buy a $1,500 power dishwasher for the kitchen and meet the median requirement of most customers. If the company bought a $30,000 high-end *super* dishwasher, the customer would not know and would not care. Appearing clean is appearing clean. The company simply spent all the extra money on something that was standard. Imagine the same high-end restaurant. You go to the restroom and enter a third-world toilet area—a hanging bulb, broken mirrors, doors without latches, and the distinct smell of...! While this type of restroom would be accepted as median at a low-rent pub, it is unacceptable in a high-end restaurant. We have median expectations that are relative to the competitive set. You could overspend on the restroom as well. Customers will not pay you more money for a restroom that costs twice that of your competitor, nor show up more often because of the elegant sinks. Exceeding the median expectation for standard elements of the business is simply wasted money.

This is the *key* to repurposing money and managerial time in an organization. Anything that is standard needs to be done and done well, but no better than the median.

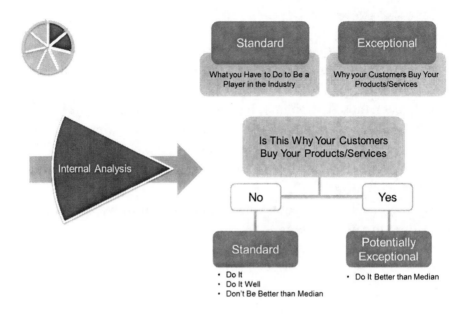

The second step is to consider why customers buy from the company. Ultimately, we are looking for the few resources or capabilities that will encourage our customers to bypass our competitors and pay us more money. These are the elements that will constitute our competitive advantage.

At this point in the effort, it is more important to list everything that anyone believes *might* be a competitive advantage. List all of those elements. In the next chapter, we will use a modified version of resource-based analysis to examine each resource or capability that you believe might be a competitive advantage in order to figure out which of those are *really* competitive advantages.

Once you have your list of potential exceptional elements, everything else falls into the standard category. If you have standard elements where the organization is significantly below the median for the industry, then all of those must be brought up to median before any real effort is put into figuring out what might be exceptional.

A world-renowned chef will be negated by dirty silverware or a sub-par restroom. What quality of pen needs to be at the table in a bank? Apparently, not very good ones. A bank that decides to put out Mont Blanc pens for customers to use will not only lose a lot of pens (no chain will hold back those customers), but also will have spent a lot of money on something that customers consider standard. By the same token, constantly having pens with no ink or not providing pens might cause customers to look elsewhere and not even pay attention to the high rates that bank is offering.

Moving this list from potentially exceptional to truly exceptional is the focus of the next chapter.

Chapter 5

A MODIFIED VERSION OF RESOURCE-BASED ANALYSIS

Resource-based analysis (and its many variations, called VRIN or VRIST or half a dozen less popular names) has been the predominant method for determining true competitive advantages since the early 1990s. It, or some version of the approach, has been around since the 1930s, but it was the move from the theoretical to the practical that really changed the fortunes of so many companies.

Many years ago we modified the approach to make it more easily applicable to businesses. We've further modified the approach to take into account the realities of busy business executives. We flipped the theoretical model on its head, as our consulting work repeatedly showed that there was no need to determine how to attain value unless the resource or capability had already passed through the other four elements. Despite the desires of most of the consulting companies, this approach to designing a strategy is really not that complicated.

The five elements of our modified version of resource-based analysis are the answers to whether the resource or capability that you think might actually separate you in the market is:

1) Rare
2) Durable
3) Relatively nonsubstitutable
4) Relatively nontradable
5) Valuable

A resource or capability has to pass all five tests for it to be a true competitive advantage.

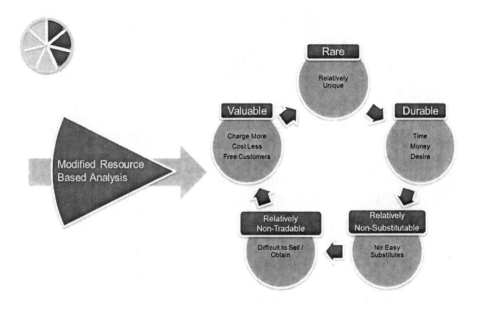

Rare

What is rare? It is an evaluation of a particular resource or capability that you believe might be potentially exceptional. It requires an honest evaluation of whether the team believes that it is really unique when compared to the comparison competitive set. The rule of thumb in the application is that if one other competitor is doing the exact same thing as your organization (and even doing it just as well), we still consider it rare. If more than one is doing so, then we fail it at this step.

Resources and capabilities have to be unique (or relatively so) for our organization to have an opportunity to enjoy extraordinary returns.

Customers will not reward you with extraordinary returns for doing the standard, expected elements of a business.

The evaluation of whether a particular resource or capability is rare should be done both quantitatively and qualitatively. Practical, real data on what a competitor is doing go a long way to answering this question. However, customers use many criteria in their evaluation of your competitors. Some of this evaluation (maybe most) is a relative evaluation of unquantifiable resources or capabilities (some real and some perceived). The management team needs to discuss these in their evaluation of whether some element is rare.

By definition, if something fails at being rare, then it is standard, and we know what to do with it (do it and do it well, but you don't need to do it any better than the median expectation of the customer).

> **Fails**—It is standard.
> **Passes**—Move on to evaluate durability.

Durable

Evaluating whether you believe that a resource or capability is relatively unique compared to your competitors is not only a crucial first step; it is also the step where most things fail. If it passes, then we need to examine whether it is durable. That is, will we be able to hold on to this rare resource or capability for long enough to make extraordinary returns? A new idea or an existing resource or capability is only of value if the organization can capitalize on it to improve the economic situation of the business.

Durability has three aspects to it:

1) Time
2) Money
3) Desire

All three are viewed from the perspective of the competitors trying to capture your customers, and while all three fundamentally translate into a time lag, each should be considered separately. Passing any one of these elements means that the resource or capability you are examining is durable. If it is durable, we move on in the analysis. If it fails at all three of these elements, then it is not durable and is no longer a potential competitive advantage.

Time—How long might it take for a competitor to match or exceed your position? This is a judgment call by management, but it should be informed by the experience and knowledge of the management team. This time frame should be set with an explanation and a general agreement from the group. Every industry is different, and that means that what constitutes an acceptable time frame will vary. In the online women's clothing industry, the time frame for something to be considered durable is quite short, while in the offshore oil gasket industry, the time frames are very long.

You are trying to estimate how long you might be able to capitalize on this unique resource or capability (which passed the rareness test earlier). Much like a project projection chart, we tend to display this on a two-dimensional chart.

The horizontal axis is time, and the vertical access is money. If we have something that we believe is rare at the current time, then it is incumbent upon the management team to estimate how long they will be able to hold on to that uniqueness. This is just an estimate, but again, it should be crafted by a knowledgeable management team.

If we are trying to create or consider something new for our organization, then we can estimate the amount of money that we will be investing (although companies are notorious for not accounting effectively for people's time in these estimates). That baseline is then modified by the required rate of return for the organization (or hurdle rate or IRR or whatever the company likes to call it). We need to be able to exceed that line before one of our competitors enters the market.

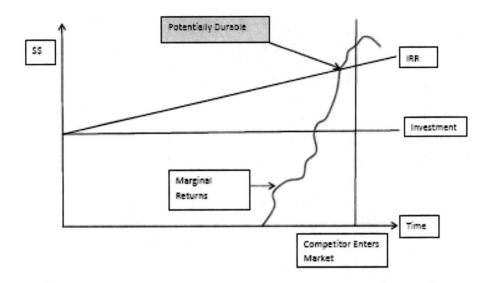

Strategists care about returns—not sales. You should estimate how long it will take from the decision to invest to the point where the company will achieve its first sales. Then estimate the potential *marginal returns* for each sale—that is, the net returns received by the company that are over and above the total variable costs of the new product or service.

If we estimate that one of our competitors will enter the market prior to our marginal returns exceeding the required rate of return line, then what we are considering is not durable from a time perspective. While returns certainly don't plummet, they do start plateauing and then dropping as new entrants capture value.

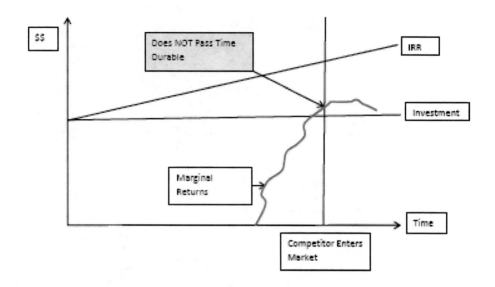

Money—If the management team determines that they will be able to hold on to the rare resource or capability for a period of time that allows for returns that exceed the required rate of return, then we must consider whether the competitors have the resources to match or exceed the resource or capability.

This is simply an estimate of whether you believe the competitor has the ability to make the investment. Due to poor business conditions, poor management decisions in the past, a weak set of financials, a bureaucracy that prevents fast following (they are convinced they are right, and no amount of data will change that thought—think Blackberry), operations mired in systems that won't allow for easy changes, or a focus on a different market segment, the company may simply not be in a position to make the required investment to match you. While this look at your competitors logically bleeds over into time (how long it would take them) and desire (whether they even think you are right), we try to separate the look in order to thoroughly open our eyes to the competitive threat.

Desire—The last of the three aspects of durability is the willingness of the competitors to try and match you. Are the competitors even interested in pursuing the RBA that you have (or are considering)? Competitors are (or should be) watching what you do and how you do what you do. The best thing that can happen for your company is for the competitor to think you are doing something that they would not even consider. That lack of desire to follow you translates into more time to enjoy the fruits of the competitive advantage.

Sprint moved aggressively to offer customers the chance to upgrade their phones twice a year when their primary competitors (Verizon and AT&T) had established the principle of phone replacement every other year. The bet by Sprint was that those companies had no desire to follow Sprint into that world. After fuming about the decision and complaining about the Sprint moves, they partially followed by allowing consumers to trade in more quickly (at a substantial cost). That lack of desire creates a time lag that may translate into a sufficient window for you to achieve extraordinary returns. In this case the competitors had the resources to invest in this approach and it would not take long to change their systems to accommodate. However, they had no desire to do so. This would pass the durable test.

What do you do with something that is rare but not durable? This depends on whether the resource or capability is one that you have now or something that you are considering doing. If it something that you have now, continue to do it until your competitors actually match you. Be careful not to tie too much of the future of the organization on something that your competitors can easily match, but enjoy what you have while you have it. If this is something that you are considering doing because no one in the industry is doing it right now (it is exciting and new)—*don't do it!* These types of creative, innovative ideas happen all the time. They are only of strategic value if you can hold on to the uniqueness for some period of time (you have to decide how long is long enough). Why increase your expenses, plow the road with customers, show competitors how to do something, and raise the bar if you cannot hold that bar for a period of time that will result in extraordinary returns? You don't. Put it in a file somewhere, and wait for your competitor to do it (whatever it is). At that point you can simply match their offering and eliminate their potential competitive advantage.

Sun Tzu's *The Art of War* tells us that a key to success is the elimination of the competitors' advantages by the simplest means possible, so that our competitive advantages will be able to win the day. At some point, one of your competitors will do a SWOT analysis and come up with this same idea (remember, they are just as smart as you and are thinking about all the same things…we just hope that they are not as sophisticated in their strategy approach). When they do, they will tout it as next best thing in the industry. You will know that this "thing" they are pitching has no durability, so dust off your files and bring it out. You will make whatever your competitor just did standard in the industry.

Relatively Nonsubstitutable

If the potential competitive advantage has passed as rare and durable, you are through the most important elements of the analysis. Most resources and capabilities fail at these two stages. The next two elements are easier to consider, and their evaluation is significantly more subjective (as if the first two were not sufficiently subjective for you!). The next two elements (Nonsubstitutable and Nontradable) examine companies that are not in our comparison competitive set. We have already examined the direct competitors with rare and durable.

There is a substitute (usually many) for every resource or capability that any company has or will ever have. If there were truly no substitutes, you would have 100 percent of the market. Noncore competitors would never have a sale. Substitutes are simply other ways that a customer attempts to attain a similar "value proposition."

The key to this element is to put yourself in the chair of your customer and consider the alternatives. The unique aspect of this look is to consider alternatives that are offered by those companies that are *not* in your comparison competitive set. You have already examined the competitors (rare and durable); now the effort turns outside the direct competitors.

How else can the customer attain some similar value to the resource or capability you are considering? The second part of this examination is whether you believe that these are good substitutes or not. There is no further science to this. You can do customer studies to gain some insight, but at the end of the day, the management team needs to decide that they believe the substitute is either good or not good.

If there is a very good substitute available in the market, then this is not a competitive advantage. Once again, if you are currently doing it, you should continue to do so. If you are considering it, you should probably stop considering it and move on to other resources or capabilities— I say "probably" because this call is quite subjective.

Take a look at how this might work. The business world is all abuzz about social networking. A company takes a look at their comparison competitive set and decides to engage in a full-on social networking blitz. They set up Twitter accounts, create customer and supplier blogs, start a series of podcasts, start video-sharing, run a rating service, and develop comprehensive data mash-ups. The effort is substantial and focused. None of their comparison competitive set is doing much more than the most basic types of social networking—it passes as rare. The time to craft a comprehensive approach is significant but not terribly long. The investment needed is substantial, but let's assume that the competitors have the resources to do this. The key is desire. Your assessment is that none of your comparison competitive set has an interest in pursuing this approach. They don't believe that it aligns with the approach they want with their customers—it passes as durable. What about nonsubstitutable? There are many substitutes for communicating with customers, suppliers, and employees—e-mail, letters, brochures, phone calls, salesman visits, advertisements, and so on. Do you believe that these substitutes—many of which have been around as long as businesses have been businesses—are good substitutes for the new social networking blitz contemplated by the company? If they are, then this fails at nonsubstitutability, and you move on to another potential resource or capability. If the management team believes that these are not effective substitutes, then you move on to the next element in the model. Is it relatively nontradable?

Relatively Nontradable

If the resource or capability has been determined by the management team to be rare, durable, and relatively nonsubstitutable, then it is incumbent upon the team to determine if it is relatively nontradable. Tradability has to do with how easy it would be for your competitors to obtain the resource or capability from *you* and whether it is something that you even have the ability to trade.

This may sound a bit strange at first. Why would you sell something that is already determined to be rare, durable, and relatively nonsubstitutable? Companies do it all the time, often for very logical reasons. If your company can sell something and *not* tear the organization apart in the process, then it may provide cash to refocus the company or change the direction of the organization. This is why many companies set up independent and autonomous business units. Doing so provides the overall organization the ability to sell off that unit without destroying the company.

I usually put this whole element into perspective. Remember that the resource or capability that you are considering has already passed as durable. Therefore, you have ruled out most of the obvious considerations of whether the resource or capability can be obtained in the open market (a product, a consulting service, or a piece of equipment, for instance). The part that you have not considered is whether your company can easily trade whatever it is to a competitor.

Here are several potential answers to the question you should ask:

Is it tradable?	"Not without losing the essence of our company!" Then move on in your analysis. This *passes*. You will not sell it. (Coke is not about to allow other companies to use their Coca-Cola formula.)
Is it tradable?	"We hold the patent on the IP, product, etc." It depends on whether you believe that the patent is

tied to the essence of your company. If it is, then move on. This *passes*. You control it and won't let it go. If it is not, then you can choose to sell it or not. (Clear Collar holds the patent on transparent cervical collars. Selling the patent would shut down the business.)

Is it tradable?   "We have an exclusive license for X amount of time." Then move on in your analysis. This *passes*. You control it and most likely can't sell it! (An exclusive license to sell a product in North America for the next ten years cannot generally be sold to another company. It is not yours to sell.)

Is it tradable?   "We don't own the concept!" This is the tricky one. If you have passed it thus far (and this is the big question with this particular aspect), *and* you can't control others using it, then this *passes*. (Offering breakfast items all day long at a fast-food chain is a concept that the fast-food chain does not own or control.) If for some bizarre reason you have passed this through the first three elements (and durability is a tough sell here), then you pass it through this element and see if you can find value. *Many times, a concept will fail at durability.*

Is it tradable?   "We bought it from another vendor!" Then you are done. This *fails*. You can't control its distribution to your competitors. You should have failed it in durability already! (We have the fastest car wash conveyor in our area. Unfortunately, we bought it from a vendor that would gladly sell it to any of our competitors.)

Is it tradable?   "We have the particular resource or capability set up as a unique business entity." Then you are done. This *fails.* You can trade it away. It is not that it is a good or a bad; it is simply that you don't want to hang your strategy hat on something that the next CEO can simply sell. (We have a large product line set up as a wholly owned subsidiary. It is easy to sell as a unit.)

Valuable

Having used this approach with hundreds of companies, I find it interesting that the classic resource-based approach starts with value. Two decades ago, I used that classic approach. The company executives would grind through the process of finding value for every resource and capability that they thought might be exceptional, only to have one after another fail at rareness. My experience with this approach has been that most things fail at rare, next most at durability, next at nonsubstitutability, and finally at nontradability. I can see no reason for executives to spend their time evaluating whether a particular resource or capability is valuable unless it actually can get to the value evaluation.

We've studied value up one side and back down the other. There are really only three ways to attain value. You charge more, it costs you less, or you draw in so-called free customers.

I am a "charge more" kind of person. If you have something that is simultaneously rare, durable, relatively nonsubstitutable, and relatively nontradable, then why would you not charge more for it? Over and over, I'm told, "We can't charge more because we are in a dog-eat-dog business. If we raise our prices, we will lose sales." If what you have has truly passed the previous elements, then charging more should be a practical and realistic goal.

If you can't charge more, for whatever reason, then you may be able to attain value because it costs you less than your competitors. Your company would get the benefit of a better basis-point run by having a lower-cost structure. This comes about for a variety of reasons, including administrative culture (ability to make decisions faster), historical artifact (your facilities are located in lower-cost environments), process issues (the company investments in process efforts have led to a more efficient operation), and a knowledge-based approach (your organization has been able to develop an approach that incorporates experience-based learning). Whatever the reason, the ability to have a resource or capability at a lower cost will provide competitive value for the organization.

The final means of attaining value is the ability to draw in "free" customers. That is, having the particular resource or capability encourages customers to bypass your competitors and do business with your company. It is the ability to draw in customers that you have not had before that propels your company's growth. The trifecta is to be able to do all three. Charge more, have it cost you less, and draw in customers that you never had before. However, if it passes for any one of these three value elements, then it passes our modified version of resource-based analysis.

Those current resources and capabilities that pass all five elements constitute the start of the sustainable competitive advantages for the organization. We always start with where the organization is *now*. Then the company should move to evaluate new resources and capabilities with the same model.

Chapter 6

SUSTAINABLE COMPETITIVE ADVANTAGES

Once the company has determined the resources and capabilities that they currently have as an organization, it is imperative that the organization use the same approach to craft and assess new ideas for the business. All this must be completed before we talk about how to implant this in the organization.

Think about the many companies that have seemingly evaluated new, bold moves only to have them blow up. Even though something might pass our modified RBA, it is not a guarantee of success; it is simply an effort to add some significant science to a process that could use a little science.

When Ron Johnson was hired away from Apple to run JCPenney, it was assumed that he would bring some creative, unique thinking to an old line retailer. He did that, but in the process he allowed his creative flair to take him well beyond what could plausibly be considered competitive advantages in the eyes of his perfect customers. Let's take a look at a couple of his ideas.

JCPenney

Assume that the comparison competitive set for JCPenney is Macy's, Target, Kohl's, and maybe Sears (if we are generous). Also assume that the perfect customer is a mom looking for bargain but also quality clothes for her family. Remember that how you set these elements dictates much of the strategy work done afterward. I'm establishing this for the discussion that follows.

Potential RBA[3] #1—Elimination of house brands in favor of name brands from Martha Stewart and Joe Fresh.

Rare? Yes. All the competitors have a mix of house brands alongside so-called name brands.

Durable? Yes. The other companies all have the financial resources to pursue the same approach. While it would take some time to eliminate the house brands and institute this on a company-wide basis, it is doable within a reasonable time frame. The only caveat might be the exclusivity of the contracts. Interestingly, none of the competitors shows any interest in pursuing this approach. The comparison competitive set make a significant amount of money (better returns) by selling house brands and have no real interest in going backward (from their perspective).

Relatively nonsubstitutable? No. There are many effective substitutes for this. There are stores that specialize in name-brand merchandise at reasonable prices (Dillard's, Belk, Stein Mart, Marshalls, and even TJMaxx, among others). This *fails* at this point, and we would *stop* the analysis. However, for argument's sake, let's suggest that you disagree with me and believe that these substitutes are not good ones. You pass it and move on.

Relatively nontradable? Yes. This approach is a concept, and JCPenney does not own the concept. Therefore, it is relatively nontradable. They don't own it to trade it! This passes.

Valuable? Could JCPenney charge more? Yes and no. The name brands certainly could be sold for more, but this ignores the significant drop in sales that might occur with the higher priced clothes. Cost less? No. These contracts will have higher costs than the house brands. Free customers? Maybe. The plan was to draw in customers who were looking for specific name brands. So, if the company could attain the aforemen-

---

3   Note that we use RBA to represent the tool Resource-Based Analysis as well as the individual perceived and actual competitive advantages with Resource-Based Advantages.

tioned exclusive contracts, then they might draw in new customers, but perhaps at the cost of some of their current customers.

Conclusion: I would have failed it at nonsubstitutability. However, a case can be made to pass it all the way through (which Ron Johnson obviously did).

Potential RBA #2—Scrapping the pricing policy of marking up prices and then offering discounts with lots of promotions and coupons.

Rare? Yes. None of the competitors were doing this. Competitors have a long history of coupons, sales, and bargain racks that they view as core to their business model.

Durable? Yes. The other companies all have the financial resources to pursue the same approach. However, it would take some time to develop the model and institute it on a company-wide basis. The time to do this would not be onerous, but none of the competitors show any interest in pursuing this approach. Investments have been made that increase competitors' reliance on sales and coupons (extending Black Friday hours).

Relatively nonsubstitutable? No. The substitutes include online retailers offering set prices without advertising or coupons and companies like Walmart that offer "low prices every day." Another substitute would potentially be flash sale sites or simply companies that continue to offer coupons. This *fails* at this point, and we would stop the analysis. However, again let's suggest that you disagree with me and believe that these substitutes are not good ones. You pass it and move on.

Relatively nontradable? Yes. It is a concept that JCPenney does not own and cannot control. Therefore, it is relatively nontradable.

Valuable? Could JCPenney charge more? No. They dramatically lowered prices, but they hoped to achieve the same true returns. Cost less? Could be. They were hoping for significant savings by eliminating the coupons, eliminating the staff that ran more than nine hundred promotions a year, and eliminating the staff to change items in the stores. Free customers? Maybe. The plan was to draw in customers who were tired of having to search for bargains and wanted a fair or consistent price—similar to the CarMax approach.

Conclusion: I would have failed it at nonsubstitutability. However, a case can be made to pass it all the way through (which Ron Johnson obviously did). I may not have mentioned this before, but I love strategy. There is *no* "right" answer. This is all interpretation. What I would like to add to the mix is a well-tested approach that requires management to evaluate a decision from many angles prior to implementation. However, as I stated early on in this book, there is a lot of art to strategy. When a decision has to be made, science can only take you so far; you must make a decision. Each executive is either good at the art or not good. I don't know how to teach art other than to provide examples and discuss implications.

The crafting of a set of true competitive advantages is critical to the success of any organization. These are the true differentiators! This is *strategy*!

Chapter 7

HAVE A REASON FOR EXISTENCE—A MISSION

Let's be honest. I believe that it is relatively fun to work through what constitutes your company's competitive advantages. It takes some discipline and real effort on the part of the team to put aside preconceived notions of competitive advantage, along with a willingness to think creatively about where the company has true advantages. However, it is the fun part of strategy. It is much easier to figure out what you should do than it is to actually do it. Far more people plan out an exercise regimen than actually follow through with the effort!

Implementation of strategy consumes the rest of this book. It is difficult and frustrating to implement a strategy, but without it there is mediocrity or worse.

Getting all or even most of the individuals in an organization to move in generally the same direction is infinitely more difficult than the old EDS commercial that extolled the virtues of herding ten thousand cats across the open plains! I firmly believe that the majority of the employees at any organization go to work every day with the intention of working hard, doing something of real value for their company, and finding a personal or professional sense of accomplishment. The real question that should be asked is "Does the team running the company have any idea of what they wish their employees to accomplish?" I believe that the resounding answer with many companies is *no*!

Why is your company in business? While it is probably to make money, this most certainly is not the reason that customers purchase anything from the organization. Customers will never (unless you are very good at begging) purchase a product or service because the company needs to make money.

Imagine this mission statement: "As our fiduciary responsibility is to maximize shareholder value, we strive to make the most money possible within the legal restraints of the countries within which we do business."

Interestingly, everyone in the company would understand that their job was to pursue any type of business activity that was legal. The employees would explain to customers, suppliers, and fellow employees that the company is trying to make as much money as possible, which is why they are charging more, requiring pay concessions, demanding reduced prices for raw materials, etc. It is not their fault; they are simply following the mission. Furthermore, everything in the known universe would be on the table for consideration. The company would have the flexibility to morph into anything it desired, regardless of its current direction or capability.

If you have done a good job developing your competitive advantages, as discussed in the previous chapters, then those advantages should be the cornerstone of why customers buy your product or service.

Simply stated—the reason that companies are in business is to provide a needed or desired product or service to a group of consumers willing to profitably compensate the company for that product or service.

Once you have developed your true competitive advantages, it is the job of the senior leadership team to get everyone in the company moving in somewhat the same direction. To start that effort, there are several elements that must be addressed:

1) The mission of the organization
2) The metrics used to measure progress
3) The fit of the organization to the strategy

Mission

The first step in the implementation effort is designing the mission statement for the organization. Rather than getting hung up on the term used (mission, vision, goal, intent, etc.), I suggest that it is the result that is critical. I have chosen to call it the mission.

A mission statement has a unique ability to focus the efforts of every employee in the company if and only if it is designed well and is implemented with a singular focus that places it above all the daily firefights at the company. Doing "good" in the typical employee's day is insufficient for the firm to truly set itself apart from the rest of its competitors. What one employee believes is "good" may exactly counter another employee's interpretation of "good." On even a small scale, this creates a situation where everyone is working extremely hard, and yet the firm seems to constantly achieve only average returns.

The goal of strategy is to achieve extraordinary returns within the company's industry. I have been examining mission statements for the past two decades and have concluded that they tend to fall into five categories. Take a look at the various types of missions that are provided to employees at many companies today, and you quickly realize why the cats are running all over the place.

Remember: It is not that the cats are doing anything inherently wrong; they are just being cats, and they will not get to any "end" as a group unless they are given a goal, a reason, and a reward.

Mission Statement Type	Implied Goal	Employee Reaction
1. The well-designed mission statement.	Senior management knows where they are taking the organization and works with employees to keep it topmost in their minds.	Empowerment! Employees have a tangible direction.
2. The "We finally have a mission statement—now get back to work."	This mission thing is not very important. Just make money. We put this out for the public and the analysts. It is full of words that no one can really disagree with!	Embarrassment! Ask these employees about their mission, and 20 percent can tell you what it is (sort of), but they quickly admit that is not what they do each day and doesn't really matter.
3. We have no mission—would you consider a "vision," "statement of purpose," or "overarching goal"?	Specificity is just not our thing. We'd prefer to be vague.	We loosely know what we want! Good thing that this statement doesn't affect me day to day.
4. We're not sure who we are, but we have "values."	As long as our employees honor these values, we can do anything.	Confusion! Corporate assets are continually spent in an attempt to define the value concepts, while the company spends inordinate efforts to examine all possibilities for growth.
5. Statements might restrict our options, so we have none.	We'll do anything to make money, increase market share, or grow the company.	Desperation! Company resources are poured into any possibility for growth.

The Importance of Direction

An organization of people exists to accomplish what the individual cannot accomplish alone. The most pressing issue that develops as the organization grows is one of coordination. As Henry Mintzberg pointed out many years ago in his definitive book on structuring organizations, the issue of coordination is the continual struggle to get employee effort focused on the unique mission of the organization.

Once you have figured out what constitutes the competitive advantages for the organization, the implementation of that strategy (the competitive advantages) logically begins with a useful, focused mission grounded in those advantages that every individual in the company can use to make decisions. Well-trained, motivated employees absent an effective, unifying mission will head in the direction that they believe is the best for the company. This may or may not align with the focus of the top management team.

Despite all the interesting books calling for the top management of companies to be inclusive, bottoms-up, consensus-building, congenial stewards of organizations, a simple fact has remained a constant—it is the responsibility of senior management to set the direction of the organization and to ensure that everyone works in unison toward that effort. Take the responsibility to accomplish this task.

My father was a navy ship commander in the Second World War. Once he received his orders, the entire crew was put to the task of attaining success in the mission. He depended on each crew member being an expert in their particular task, and yet he also depended on all of them working together to accomplish the mission that he laid before them. Imagine, if you will, the typical corporate scenario at play aboard this naval war ship. We don't know exactly where we're going, but we want to be very efficient. We hire good people and tell them to "do good." People in each area of the ship concern themselves with improving their operations and arguing in meetings that their needs are supreme. Each area of the ship receives award after award for their outstanding performance, but the ship wanders the seas.

In a long history of looking at mission statements, researchers and practitioners have almost universally acknowledged the value of a singular mission as a driving force for companies and yet have been inconsistent in advising what a great mission statement might look like. An effective mission statement needs to not only be specific to that organization; it must highlight and focus the energy of everyone in the organization in the direction that the top management team believes is best for the business. If the top management is wrong, so be it. Then the company will move quickly and decisively in the wrong direction until new leadership recognizes and corrects the mission. The core problem is not the presence or absence of a mission statement; it is that far too many are unremarkable, unreadable, too long to remember, and simply not applied in the daily management of companies.

The culmination of all the studies completed in this area, along with almost twenty years of assisting companies to design effective mission statements, has led to the development of a five-point approach to creating an effective mission statement. These five points should drive the "art" of designing a quality statement.

The Five Keys to Designing a Mission Statement

1. Short: Does it fit on a coffee mug?
2. Simple: Something that everyone in the company can learn and understand.
3. Directional: Guides every individual in the company every day.
4. Actionable: Tells everyone exactly what the company does and what it does not do.
5. Measurable: Must be able to develop a metric for every part of the statement.

Keep It Short

The fun question I ask is "Does it fit on a coffee mug?" Keeping the statement short may be the single most important element of a well-designed mission statement. The mission statement is not a tome that describes everything that you have done or might do and how you will do it so that the organization can impress external sources! It is a short, direct statement that can be easily recalled by those within the organization as well as customers, suppliers, and the investing public. Some horrible historic (and not so historic) advice has stated that a mission statement should embrace all of the following elements:[4]

1) Customers
2) Products/services
3) Geographic markets
4) Technology
5) Concern for survival/growth
6) Philosophy
7) Public image
8) Employees
9) Distinctive competence

The result of this advice has been the creation of mission statements that could not be recalled by a poet laureate. An all-encompassing mission statement that cannot be easily recalled by your employees is simply an exercise in frustration, expense, and outright derision. The focus of the statement has to be the true competitive advantages of the business.

Keep It Simple

A well-designed mission statement has to be something that everyone in the organization can learn *and* understand. A mission statement

---

4   FR David and FR David, "It's Time to Redraft Your Mission Statement," *Journal of Business Strategy* 24, no. 1 (2003): 11–14; RD Ireland and MA Hitt, "Mission Statements: Importance, Challenge, and Recommendations for Development," *Business Horizons* 35, no. 3 (1992): 34–42; JA Pearce and FR David, "Corporate Mission Statements: The Bottom Line," *Academy of Management Executive* 1, no. 2 (1987): 109–116.

that is not well understood and communicated has little if any value to the organization. Spending countless hours crafting a statement only to have it poorly communicated or not reinforced by the senior management of the company also prevents all the constituents (inside and outside the company) from knowing the chosen direction of the company.

The senior management team needs to ensure that the words and concepts employed in the statement have a clear meaning to all who hear or read them. (If you saw the movie *Pirates of the Caribbean*, you may recall the entertaining language play where Captain Barbosa replies tongue in cheek to his upper-class captive, "I'm disinclined to acquiesce to your request," pauses for moment, and turns back to his captive and says, "Means '*no.*'") A good mission statement will avoid using adjectives or descriptive language about how the company will accomplish its mission. An effective mission statement is a guide, not a detailed set of instructions.

Keep It Directional

The mission has to be able to guide every individual in the company each and every day. It takes extraordinary care to develop a statement that guides the entire organization. Yet, for it to be effectively utilized by every member of the company, it must have direct applicability to even the most entry-level employee. Imagine the customer service employee who deals with customers calling in with their concerns, complaints, etc. If the mission statement of the organization is a long-winded run of concepts that fundamentally says "we do it all," or if it is like so many mission statements and simply extols the employees to "maximize shareholder value," then what is the customer service employee to do? What generally happens is that employees simply try to do their best given some mix between their own sense of "justice" and the admonishments of their immediate superior.

Keep It Actionable

In order for a mission statement to have direct, measurable impact, it has to be something that helps employees make active decisions in the moment without having to refer every decision up the chain of command. A well-developed mission statement helps ensure that everyone in the organization is heading in the same relative direction so that decisions will not be made (within some variance) that are counter to the direction that senior management has chosen. One mission statement that simultaneously achieves all four components that we have thus discussed is the one for Southwest Airlines. In it they actually define what they mean by customer service.

Southwest Airlines (2014)

The mission of Southwest Airlines is dedication to the highest quality of customer service delivered with a sense of warmth, friendliness, individual pride, and company spirit.

One of the primary goals of an effective mission statement is its ability to allow (empower) employees at all levels to use their judgment in the execution of their daily responsibilities. An effective mission statement tells everyone exactly what you *do* and therefore, by definition, what you *do not do.*

Employees are constantly faced with decisions that appear to be of little importance, but those decisions do indeed have both individual and cumulative impact. An actionable mission statement keeps everyone in the organization actively striving to achieve the goals of the top management team. The focus within the mission statement goes beyond a laundry list of areas covered in the business; instead, it should be narrowly defined as "an organization's unique and enduring purpose."[5] Consider the following:

---

5   CK Bart and MC Baetz, "The Relationship between Mission Statements and Firm Performance: An Exploratory Study," *Journal of Management Studies* 35, no. 6 (1998): 823–854.

Autoliv (2014)

To create, manufacture, and sell state-of-the-art automotive safety systems.

We know exactly what Autoliv will and will not do. If an employee is approached with an interesting new product that will improve the sound quality within the automobile, the employee knows instantly that this is outside the purview of the company. The senior management has made the decision to focus their time, energy, and resources on the creation, manufacture, and sales of state-of-the-art automotive safety systems. This focus prevents the company from wasting valuable time and resources pursuing areas outside of their core competence.

Keep It Measurable

The mission statement is only as valuable as it is practical. While all corporations have or should have a set of metrics for the organization, the metrics developed from an effective mission statement focus the company's efforts on its set of competitive advantages. Briefly stated, corporate metrics generally fall into two categories: those that are quantitative and those that are qualitative. Many companies aim to develop seven or so metrics, with four being quantitative and three being qualitative. A great check on the quality of the mission statement that you have written is your ability to design metrics that measure each and every part of the mission. Consider the following mission statement:

New York Times (2014)

Enhance society by creating, collecting, and distributing high-quality news, information, and entertainment.

This well-designed mission statement allows for the development of metrics that will provide an effective measure of their success at achieving their mission. The *New York Times* aims to do three things (create, collect, and distribute) across three areas (high-quality news, high-quality

73

information, and high-quality entertainment) in order to accomplish one goal (enhance society). All of these can then be translated into specific metrics given the top management's approach to what constitutes high quality. Examples might be as follows:

1) Number of high-quality news articles written by *NY Times* staff writers divided by the total number of news articles appearing in the *NY Times*. This could be measured daily.
2) Perception of the quality of articles in the *NY Times*. Number of awards?
3) Number of *NY Times* articles that are picked up by other news sources.

The metrics designed for the *NY Times* will be unique to that organization and truly measure how it is succeeding in its mission.

Well-Designed Mission Statements

Merck (2014)—"To discover, develop, and provide innovative products and services that save and improve lives around the world."

Dow Chemical (2014)—"To passionately create innovation for our stakeholders at the intersection of chemistry, biology, and physics."

Nike (2014)—"To bring inspiration and innovation to every athlete in the world."

Starbucks (2014)—"To inspire and nurture the human spirit—one person, one cup, and one neighborhood at a time."

Chapter 8

HOW TO MEASURE SUCCESS— METRICS AND FIT

Moving from a thoughtful strategy to a well-designed mission statement starts the process of implanting the strategy in the organization. Before moving on to the other elements of implementation, it is crucial that the organization determine what will constitute success and how it will be measured. Setting this out at the beginning of the effort ensures an understanding by everyone involved and establishes the baseline means of measuring that success.

While the metrics will be input as a part of the one-page strategy map, it is important at this point to understand the process, what constitutes an effective strategy metric, and what will drive performance in the organization. Nothing works quite so well as a well-crafted "scorecard."

Strategy metrics are designed to demonstrate that the business activities are reinforcing the competitive strategy. That is to say, in a strategy effort, we are not trying to measure classic accounting or finance metrics of performance. Those will be measured and should be measured, but they are lagging variables that are a result of the activities of the business, not the reason the business has the results.

All this effort is aligned around the issue of *fit*. There should be consistency and alignment between what we believe makes the business unique and how that is perceived by customers. Everything that is measured should reinforce the specific strategy that the business is trying to drive.

We want profits to rise, but we can't just tell employees to make it happen. Employees perform activities for the business that, if guided correctly, will lead to an increase in the post hoc measures of performance.

While all tied together, there are a number of elements that should be considered in the design of metrics.

1) Type of metrics—qualitative vs. quantitative
2) Tie to strategy
3) Use of pre- and post-measurement
4) Range, continuous vs. discrete, and goal metrics
5) Colinearity and big data

Type of Metrics—Qualitative vs. Quantitative

There is a fairly compelling argument made by many people that if you can't quantify it, then you can't measure it. While I disagree with this statement in general, it is all the more important to distance yourself from this approach when trying to measure success in strategy. There is a place in the understanding gained by the depth and context associated with the use of qualitative metrics.

Quantitative metrics: Those measures that are represented by raw numbers or are the result of statistical analysis.

Qualitative metrics: Information that is contextual in nature, representing nonnumerical measures.

Quantitative metrics are the measures or results that virtually everyone is most comfortable reporting and considering. They include the number of unique visits to our website, the percentage of customers purchasing more than one item, the average time for a new customer to enroll in our loyalty program, and so on. There is something quite reassuring about being able to identify a result and compare it directly to the result from the previous day, week, quarter, or year. These types of metrics are quite valuable, but they provide insufficient information from which to make strategy decisions. Another far more insidious issue is the way the metric is actually calculated. There is significant manipulation of most metrics (even the ones we think we understand well); therefore, the only real value is not in the measure itself but in its comparison with the previous period. The delta (change) in the metric becomes a small barometer of success.

Consider the reporting of same-store sales. The raw number is far less important than the change from the previous year. Every location has unique issues and customers. The change from the previous year helps organizations balance those issues and look at the improvement at the store level (or any more precise level of analysis). Strategists are particularly interested in comparison and change metrics. It is irrelevant to learn that sales went up by 3.4 percent without the context of what happened previously in your own operation or in comparison to your competitors. If the competition went up 8 percent, then the 3.4 percent looks terrible.

Quantitative metrics are of real value to a business; however, they only provide snapshots of information to the management team. In order to get a more complete look at the business, managers keep adding and adding quantitative metrics to their reporting. One report begets another, and the IT department staffs up to provide more and more "results" in so-called readable forms for management to evaluate the business. It is a never-ending cycle that needs to be curbed. We will discuss several techniques for the drastic reduction of data points when we talk about colinearity later in this chapter.

Qualitative metrics provide us the opportunity to fill context and understanding in between the quantitative metrics. This is especially important as we reduce the raw number of snapshot quantitative metrics that are reported. The real difficulty lies in preventing the quantification of everything that is collected.

How do you gauge what a particular customer thinks about the french fries at McDonald's versus Burger King versus Wendy's? We can ask customers to rank various aspects of our french fries, but we may not be getting at why they prefer (or don't prefer) our french fries. Listening to how customers describe the fries, what they don't like about fries, and how they feel about their fries provides a depth of understanding not easily applicable to quantification.

Developing a feel for the qualitative aspects of the business can be done in a number of ways. In the early years of his business, J. Peterman held a breakfast with eight to ten different employees every week. His only rule about what could be discussed was that there were no rules. Alan Mulally regularly sat in the back of various meetings to get a sense of how the business was progressing. It takes a hands-on approach to collect qualitative input.

Some companies hire consultants to run focus groups with customers, test the market for new ideas, and watch consumer and employee behavior. Requiring every senior manager to work the customer service lines for eight hours a quarter is a quantitative metric that will lead to spectacular qualitative insights. We can easily poke fun at shows like "Undercover Boss," but the lack of insight into the jobs that actually make the money for an organization points out how quickly one can lose touch. A method for collecting and utilizing qualitative data is a means for staying ahead of the competition.

All this is to encourage a mix between qualitative and quantitative metric collection. The reality is that we can combine the two to provide unique insights. Using techniques such as content analysis or conjoint analysis allows unique insights that have measurable metrics for use by the leadership team.

Tie to Strategy

For strategy to mean anything beyond the words on a page, it has to be evaluated in some way. What's more, the metrics used should examine the activities, not the results, that we believe will move us closer to knowing that our strategy is actually being implemented.

I have spoken with many CEOs who are frustrated that their well-designed strategy has not led to the company growth they had envisioned. With a bit of investigation, we find that we can't evaluate the success or failure of the strategy because it was never really implemented. Management teams below senior management paid lip service to the new direction but didn't change any of their actions.

Companies need a completely new set of metrics to know that the strategy is actually being implemented. Those metrics need to be tied directly to the unique strategies of the business.

STRATEGY	METRICS
Most convenient	Percentage of customers who utilize curbside drop-off Time to initial greeting Number of customers who post compliments about convenience Number of clicks to completed transaction What equates to having the most convenience in your business? Customer feedback directly complimenting aspects of convenience
Best available selection	Number of product or service categories with activity Percentage of customers who don't purchase per visit Number of items that must be specially ordered Aspects of selection from unsolicited comments
Highest expertise	Percentage of customers who ask questions Percentage of employees who have been approached by recruiters Number of times an employee must refer to outside sources Sales from experiments with high expertise and low expertise provided in specific units Secret shop-

	per reviews Customers' feelings relative to shopping at competitors
Personal connection	Number of customers who are known by their nicknames Percentage of time an employee knows the customers' orders before they order Impression of floor conversations

Note that not only are these activity metrics, but also they are all aimed toward the actions, perceptions, or responses of paying customers. If designed effectively, the change that the strategy envisions will result in a change with customers.

Use of Pre- and Postmeasurement

There is a very effective saying that I use on a regular basis with companies:

"You are what you *are*."

The company may have pitched itself as the most caring, most accurate, highest quality company in the industry, when it actually falls quite short on all of those aspects. Companies exist in the market today with reputations, customers, employees, and capabilities. The senior management may wish that the company was viewed as more innovative, cohesive, collaborative, or any of a host of concepts. However, accepting where the company is today is a great place to set the baseline of all metrics.

We worked with a large manufacturing company that claimed it had a 92 percent on-time delivery record. When working with a group of middle managers on their competitive advantages, I pushed the group to look at the processes that allowed this type of remarkable on-time delivery record in an industry that was lucky to claim 60 percent.

The senior management of the company wanted to use that 92 percent as the baseline and look to increase it to 94 percent within a year in order to keep a sizable lead over their competitors. The middle managers kept pushing back on using this as a competitive advantage, when one manager finally shared the following (paraphrased from the original):

"Well, Chuck, it really may not be 92 percent. See, if we have a problem with manufacturing, supply, delivery, or anything really, then we call the customer and let them know about the problem and reset the delivery date with their permission."

"What do you do if the customer does not give you permission?" I asked.

"Haha, well…we change it anyway because we have an issue."

"OK, then why is your on-time rate not 100 percent?" I posed to the group.

There was a long delay in the room with a lot of murmuring; then the answer finally came: "Guess we figured that senior management would not believe that number."

I went back to senior management, and we decided to shut down their ability to make changes to the scheduled delivery date once it had been entered into the system (no small feat, as IT thought we had asked for Neptune and Saturn to be switched in the solar system). After a month, it became clear that the on-time delivery record was going to be very bad. At the three-month mark, we concluded that the real on-time delivery percentage was 8 percent.

As dejecting as that was for the senior management to deal with, strategy metrics are about accepting where you are and improving on that. We set 8 percent as the baseline and started measuring performance from there. Initially, the senior management demanded that on-time delivery double (to 16 percent) within three months. This may not sound spectacular, but this metric was so far below the median in the industry—if we presume that all the other competitors were telling the truth—that it was not a potential competitive advantage (as they had hoped) but a standard that was well below the industry expectations.

You must establish premeasurements for all strategy metrics. Then set regular time periods for evaluation of each metric, and report those results.

Mean vs. Range, Continuous vs. Discrete, and Goal Metrics

There are some very common approaches to strategy metrics that need to be briefly discussed. The classic approach used by far too many folks is to examine the average (mean) or some type of raw number count as a means for tracking performance improvement. Unfortunately, both of these have flaws that can be easily manipulated, preventing management from gaining the improvements that they are seeking. While all metrics have inherent issues, average does a particular disservice, because improvements in the measure may be achieved by reducing the denominator (number of behaviors tracked) or by increasing the numerator (desired behavior), and its value gets discounted as the numbers increase—it hides problems. It does not tell us what the customer actually experiences; it only provides a gross metric for what they might be expected to experience half the time.

Range as a metric allows us to look at the improvement in the consistency of performance with the customer. We worked with a small restaurant operation that had a drive-in line. Senior management carefully monitored the speed with which a customer was served. The goal was to keep the average wait to no more than four minutes. However, a one-hour watch of the drive-in line found that customers experienced a range of performance that ran from virtually instant service (items ready when they rolled up to the window) to waiting fifteen minutes before being served. Inconsistency in *any* experience that a customer receives from your organization is a source of frustration. Consistency (as I've pointed out before) is a key to strategy success.

Consider what might have happened to the customer over ten contacts with the company:

Customer contact	1	2	3	4	5	6	7	8	9	10	AVG
Wait time to service (sec)	0	0	15	35	50	180	180	255	810	820	234.5

Now, imagine that a huge effort was made by senior management to get employees to improve the average wait time for the customer. The result might be as follows:

Customer contact	1	2	3	4	5	6	7	8	9	10	AVG
Wait time to service (sec)	0	0	0	20	70	75	75	265	905	910	232

The result was a slight decrease in the average wait time for the customer over ten visits (something that might have resulted in applause and bonuses). There was improvement in the number of times that the customer waited less than four minutes; however, the actual times when they missed the four-minute mark grew enormously.

Interviews with the employees delivering the experience revealed that they felt they knew that what management really cared about was the number of times that a customer waited for less than four minutes. Once a customer had not been helped within that window, employees simply pushed them out of the queue and sent them to a special parking spot to await their order while trying to maximize the numbers that they could serve within the window of time.

Range is a far more important metric in strategy than mean. Reducing the range of wait times that customers experience (regardless of whether the average goes up or down) allows senior management to be more confident in the consistency of implementation of the strategy.

Continuous and discrete measures of strategy allow for very different results from employees. Discrete metrics are those that are taken at points in time. They allow senior management to hold a number of extraneous factors constant while examining the movement of the metric being examined. Employees generally know when measures are being taken, and even with no malice intended, they adjust their performance. Discrete measures are of value, but they should be used in combination with continuous measures. If we assume that an organization can always improve (a fairly safe assumption), then we don't want employees to stop striving or varying their efforts. Continuous measures have no upward bound. You will notice that all the measures listed earlier in the chapter lend themselves to continuous measurement.

Goal metrics may seem to counter the comments about continuous measurement, but they are simply a reality in the operation of any company. Once we have laid out the metrics that will be used in the measurement of strategy, it is incumbent upon senior management to establish goals and time frames for each.

Colinearity and Big Data

Developing a set of metrics for the business is an important step, and inevitably, the business will collect a vast array of metrics. We've worked with a number of businesses that had an initial list of strategy metrics that ran from thirty-six to over fifty! Every tracked metric seems to have a sponsor within the company who simply cannot live without that particular piece of information. Yet we all realize that there are too many data points tracked in general. The newest buzzword, "big data," seems to imply that if we can slice up all the data available to the business, executives will be provided with "answers" that will help them grow the company.

Big data as a so-called strategy has many fallacies inherently built into the concept. The first is the issue of population data. Many executives seem to believe that if we use all the data collected by the business, there will be insights not available by using classic statistical estimation techniques. While there is a extremely small chance that this is true, it is far outweighed by the sheer cost associated with collecting, holding, managing, analyzing, and reporting the analysis. The chances of an error of estimation can be reduced to an extraordinarily small number with classical sampling. However, the biggest misconception is that these companies are really working with population data in the first place. Companies do not collect population data; they can only collect data from the population of the company's customers. It has a bias built in that provides no insight into what your competitors' customers are doing. As such, saving the expense and effort of trying to analyze millions or tens of millions of transactions is even more justified.

There is an enormous value in analyzing company "Big Data; however, it needs to be focused on the desired strategy elements of the business and needs to take into consideration the cost and time of such huge efforts. The rest is just noise.

What is the quickest and most reliable means of reducing the number of metrics being tracked? A Pearson correlation table provides insights into how relatable each metric is to each other. Without going into vast detail about the workings of the approach, suffice it to say that a Pearson correlation table (available in any spreadsheet package) will compare every variable to every other variable.

Two variables that are perfectly correlated (that is, they move together in lockstep) will have a value of 1.0 (rarely, if ever, seen). Two variables that are perfectly correlated in the opposite direction will have a value of -1.0 (also rarely seen). The table will be filled with values that lie between 1.0 and -1.0. For our purposes and for being able to use metrics in some type of predictive analysis, any number that is greater than 0.4 or less than -0.4 means that those two metrics are so highly correlated that they are effectively measuring the same thing (for the purposes of strategy implementation).

Take a look at the table above. After all the metrics are collected for a period of time (one month in this case), every metric is evaluated against every other metric with this very straightforward statistical look. The "1.00" down the diagonal simply confirms that every variable is perfectly correlated with itself. The highlighted correlations are ones that exceed our .4/-.4 threshold. These metrics are so highly related that they effectively measure the same thing. In these cases, management should choose one to collect and track while eliminating the collection and reporting of the other. Our rule of thumb is to collect the metric that is easiest to obtain and understand.

In this example:

1) Metric #2 is highly negatively correlated with metrics #3, #7, #11, and #12.
2) Metric #4 is highly positively correlated with metric #9.
3) Not surprisingly, metric #7 is highly positively correlated with metrics #11 and #12.

	Mean	s.d.	1	2	3	4	5	6	7	8	9	10	11	12	13	14	15	16
1	.208	.53	1.00															
2	.00	1.00	.01	1.00														
3	3.41	1.44	.10	-.56	1.00													
4	7.45	3.56	.24	-.18	.04	1.00												
5	.26	.17	-.05	-.47	-.20	.12	1.00											
6	.62	.40	.02	.10	.02	.08	.08	1.00										
7	.00	1.00	-.07	-.49	-.09	-.01	.26	.01	1.00									
8	3.68	1.88	-.22	.06	.41	.13	-.07	.19	-.01	1.00								
9	8.09	3.57	.23	-.16	.04	.72	.10	-.06	-.21	.23	1.00							
10	.10	.06	-.01	-.13	-.01	-.01	.14	-.01	.59	.07	-.06	1.00						
11	4.37	1.23	-.01	-.67	.20	-.06	.17	.35	.55	.48	.26	-.02	1.00					
12	3392	2450	.32	.64	-.09	.29	.21	.23	.08	.03	.09	.11	.24	1.00				
13	1982	1.09	.12	-.13	.08	.05	.11	.02	.13	.26	.23	.10	.06	.30	1.00			
14	14.68	1.88	.23	-.21	.04	.25	.11	.21	.02	.01	.13	-.02	.04	.37	.08	1.00		
15	.0051	.0087	.11	-.08	.04	-.08	.02	-.02	-.02	.01	.13	-.02	-.01	.15	.08	.04	1.00	
16	.4690	1.74	-.06	.02	-.03	.13	.02	-.05	-.02	.03	.13	-.08	-.02	-.09	-.20	-.33	-.01	1.00

Collecting metric #2 allows us to eliminate the collection of three other metrics while keeping in mind that those metrics move in the opposite direction from metric #2. We could collect either metric #4 or metric #9 but should not collect both.

This approach can and should be done over and over throughout the company's metrics in order to narrow the number collected and to allow management to focus their attention. While there is a lot to consider in the measurement of strategy, the elements that we briefly discussed in this chapter will go a long way toward ensuring that the strategy designed is being measured with activity metrics that provide insight to the senior leadership team.

Chapter 9

STRUCTURING THE ORGANIZATION SENSIBLY

There is nothing more critical in the implementation of strategy than how we organize and motivate the people in the company who will make that strategy a reality.

Want to shut down the work in your company? Just mention that there might be a reorganization. Whom one reports to on a daily basis is a contentious issue in any organization. I have found that people are all-in with developing strategy until you get to this aspect of the implementation and talk about reorganizing the business. At that point, they want to distance themselves from the effort. This reluctance comes not only from the nature of reporting to someone new, but also from a long, long history of reorganizations that have "arbitrary" written all over them.

Every manager we talk with seems to have his or her own approach to how the business should be organized. These approaches are bound in the manager's "theory of the business" and lead to structures that might or might not advance the strategy of the business. When employees don't understand why a structure has been put in place or how it will work with the strategy, then the whole effort is undermined.

The long, hard truth of outstanding company performance is that structure follows strategy. Once you have developed your competitive advantages, it is imperative that you structure the business around those advantages. Every single textbook on strategy has a chapter on the forms of structure that are presented (with lovely charts) and describe the meta-approaches to the topic. These include terms like the following:

1) Functional
2) Divisional
3) Geographic
4) Multidomestic
5) Network
6) Matrix

The list goes on and on. All of these global approaches describe an overall approach that has little to do with the design and implementation of strategy. We leave all these diagrams and the associated descriptions to the textbooks and spend the time we have in this book to address a very practical approach to looking at the company and restructuring the business to match the strategy. Structuring a business is *hard*, and it takes a lot of work to keep it relevant.

The Goal of Structuring the Organization

To effectively deliver on the strategic differentiation of the company in a manner that has the fewest possible layers between the CEO and the lowest-level worker.

This means that each leader must be able to effectively deliver results while directing as many employees as possible. That simply cannot be accomplished by just adding people to a particular manager. We need a means by which we can effectively direct large numbers of people in the organization.

Henry Mintzberg wrote the most applicable and insightful look at the subject in his book *The Structuring of Organizations*.[6] While there has been a lot of work on this topic since this book, the book stands strong for managers looking for a meaningful way to structure their company. Once a strategy is in place, a mission has been crafted, and the strategy metrics have been designed, it is incumbent on the managers to structure the business to make the most of this effort. The

---

6   Henry Mintzberg, *The Structuring of Organizations* (Englewood Cliffs, NJ: Prentice Hall, 1979).

approach that is discussed below uses Mintzberg as its foundation and incorporates the latest practical (as opposed to experimental) knowledge in the field.

With the exception of executive management, every person working in an organization can be categorized as belonging to one of three elements or areas of the business:

a. Strategy core
b. In-house advisors and policy makers
c. Operations

Each of those areas needs to be coordinated. There are four fundamental approaches, with a fifth that is still being debated. The goal of the coordination method chosen is to maximize the number of employees that can be managed by a single manager or leader while achieving the goals of the organization. The coordination approaches are as follows:

a. Mutual team adjustment
b. Standardization of work processes
c. Standardization of worker skills
d. Standardization of work output
e. Standardization of business norms

Three Areas of Any Organization

As we stated above, every individual in an organization can be effectively divided into one of three areas. The *strategy core* is that group or groups that are most responsible for the competitive advantages of the business. The core needs to have *in-house advisors* (experts) and *policy makers* (protectors). Advisors are specialists that assist the core group or groups as they push the competitive advantages of the business forward. Policy makers protect the organization by ensuring that policies and procedures are in place and are followed as required by regulators, business practices, laws, and the desires of senior managers. The *operations* groups are those charged with most of the standard (orthodox) elements of the business.

There is no perfect way to organize a business, but how it is organized will make a huge difference in its ability to deliver on its stated strategy. Now that we have established the foundations for structuring the organization, let's take a look at a business and contemplate how it might be organized.

Consider a fairly typical fast-food restaurant in the United States. The restaurant has dozens (maybe hundreds) of standard operational elements. It has a counter, tables, chairs, napkins, a cash register, a soda machine, a menu display board, fryers, some type of assembly line for food preparation and cooking, display cases, refrigerators, freezers, trash cans, air conditioning and heating, procedures for preparing food, cleaning requirements, methods of reporting sales and costs, and so on.

As has been discussed a number of times, all of these standard elements of the business need to be done and done well, but they don't need to be done any better than the competition unless some element is being crafted as a true competitive advantage. We want to supply napkins for our customers, but we only need to supply average napkins. Too high a quality and they will start disappearing in large numbers; too low a quality and customers will complain or never come back. Ketchup is an expectation (at least in the U.S.), but what quality allows the restaurant to minimize costs without losing sales? These standard elements are critical to the running of the business, but they are not the reason that the customer has chosen this particular fast-food restaurant over the dozens of others.

Every element that was just listed (and many more) is the responsibility of the various operations functions. We want to organize the business such that all the *standard* elements of the business are handled by a group or groups whose entire job is to maintain an acceptable level of performance that is equal (or close to equal) to our direct competitors.

For the sake of this discussion, let's presume that the true competitive advantages of this fast-food restaurant are (1) a 24-7 operation where the customer can have breakfast or regular food items anytime; and (2) a private dining area where no cell phone may be used and where no talking is allowed.

In this case one of the strategy core groups would be focused on the specific requirements of each restaurant in order for it to make every type of food offered twenty-four hours a day. The procedures, logistics, and handling that will ensure that this element of the strategy can be delivered are core to the success of the business. Another strategy core group would be focused on the design of a private area within each and every location as well as procedures to ensure that it remains true to the offering. Refining and continuous improvement of these two competitive advantages need to be the full-time job of a core group of individuals.

In-house advisors and policy makers round out the design of the business. They play a central role between the standard and the exceptional elements of the business. Advisors might be engineering, mechanical, menu designers, logistics, and legal groups, whereas human resources, accounting, and store operations might be logically placed in the policy maker role. Policy makers have the power to protect the organization by setting appropriate policies and provide it with consistency, whereas advisors provide specialized information and expertise within the company to help the core make better decisions. The reason that these two groups are bound together is that there is crossover in each group's responsibilities. In-house advisors also set some policies, and in-house policy makers also provide advice to the strategy core groups.

Virtually any group can be categorized as operations, in-house advisors, or in-house policy makers. The way you craft which group falls into which category determines their roles in the organization. As was stated before, there is no "right" way to structure an organization; however, by applying a bit of the "science" of strategy, you can establish a focus on the elements that truly differentiate the company.

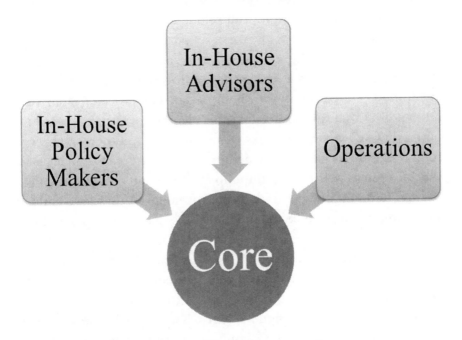

Four (Maybe Five) Coordination Approaches

Once each of the areas within the company has been categorized into strategy core, in-house advisors, policy makers, and operations, we can turn our attention to how we coordinate employees' work within each group. Every person in a business ultimately ends up in some type of direct supervision reporting relationship. The goal remains the same; we wish to achieve a situation where we can manage large groups of people with a single manager or leader.

Notwithstanding the fun articles we read in the papers about companies trying out structureless business approaches, the reality is that there are very few if any businesses that operate effectively in the long run without some version of a reporting system. Success in strategy implementation is about how to coordinate, evaluate, and manage internal work groups.

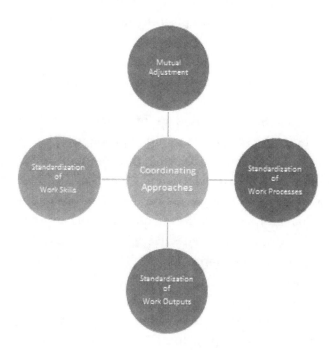

As was mentioned before, there are really only four coordinating approaches—we will discuss the potential fifth one separately. The first one on the list gets the closest to the current fad approach of a structure-less business, but it operates within a direct supervision structure on some level.

Mutual Adjustment

Mutual adjustment is a coordination approach putting together a group of people (who ultimately have to report their results to someone) without an internal reporting structure in order to accomplish a task. The approach works best when

- Groups are small,
- The need is very well defined,
- The means to answer that need is unknown, or
- The time frame to accomplish the task is very short.

In this approach, there is no one in a supervisory role on the team. The team sets the rules, and the team is jointly responsible for the outcome.

This approach has been used quite effectively by "skunk works" groups to find creative solutions to unique problems. The approach was made famous by Lockheed-Martin when the company pulled a group of people together in 1943 to develop a jet fighter. Steve Jobs used the same approach to create the McIntosh. Generally accomplished by separating the group from the hierarchy of the company, this approach to group coordination is extraordinarily effective. Time is not taken out for meetings, status reports, budget approvals, etc. The method focuses everyone on a task and works well as long as the aforementioned criterion is well adhered to by the company.

Mutual adjustment has not been found to work with ongoing business needs and does not appear to have any value when the group size increases beyond the point where everyone can be in the same area working together. There is something to love about getting virtually 100 percent of employees' time focused on a solution, but the reality is that this coordination approach has limited uses.

Any area where we can utilize mutual adjustment is a bonus. If that approach won't work, then the effort needs to shift to some form of structural standardization. The more we can standardize the work, the more people that can be effectively coordinated. There is no particular order to which area works best or should be considered first. However, I generally start with processes, move to skills, and finally resort to outputs.

Standardization of Work Processes

When a new company starts out, everything that happens is a new experience for the employees and the company as a whole. There is no "company memory" and no real processes for handling the operations of the company. I worked with a client that had grown to over $10 million in sales and yet did not have a standard onboarding process for new clients (not a good thing). Virtually the only way for a company to achieve any real size is for it to standardize processes wherever possible so that the mental firepower of employees is reserved for unusual situations.

Every aspect of the standard parts of the business can be considered a candidate for a process approach, as can some aspects of every part of the business. The goal of this approach is for managers to direct and evaluate adherence to the process.

Once the engineers have designed the machinery and flow for cigarettes to be made in a plant, the small number of employees required to run that machinery are there to ensure that the process works as designed. The plant management can and should focus on the processes. As long as the employees are adhering to the processes, all should work well. We certainly look for employees to recommend improvements and inform management when something is not working as planned, but fundamentally, the management team is there to ensure that the processes are being followed. Don't take this wrong, but it does not really matter who the actual employee is at each part of the process.

I've seen processes in virtually every aspect of companies. The factory or plant setting is obvious, as are areas of insurance companies that process new applications, paralegals handling real estate closings, wait staff at most restaurants, residential lawn-care teams, dry cleaners, the towel-drying crews at full-service car washes, and so on. Every company has vast aspects that can be controlled by processes and procedures. We want to organize those into logical groups so that managers and leaders in those areas can coordinate the work of dozens or hundreds of employees at a time. The question that is constantly asked with this coordination approach is, "Is the employee effectively following the process or procedure that is in place?"

Standardization of Work Skills

When mutual adjustment is not appropriate and the work of the employees simply defies standardization of the processes, then we look to see if there is a group or a set of groups that can be managed based on their skill set. There are both formal and informal skill sets that provide the opportunity to manage large numbers of employees.

Formal skill sets include outside certifications (CPA, MD, JD, MBA, dental hygienist, court stenographer, and Six Sigma). These are designations that suggest that everyone who has earned the certification has a base level of knowledge and nomenclature that is consistent across individuals with these designations. These folks can talk to each other using acronyms that shorten the whole process of communication. Furthermore, they tend to have a common code of conduct that one can rely upon. That said, we all can recount instances where this trust was violated. Coordinating the work activities by skill set does not absolve the manager of the responsibility to evaluate and correct performance. It does provide a powerful way to manage lots of people.

The big consulting firms like to hire MBAs from a restricted set of schools so that they know exactly what and how their employees have been taught. The consultants are expected to have a set of skills that can then be refined and sent out in large numbers to far-flung companies.

There are also a great number of more informal skill sets that allow for this same approach. In a typical large auto dealership, there is a group of mechanics to work on vehicles. While mechanics go through a series of in-house and vendor-run courses, the expectation is that everyone has a basic automotive skill set such that fundamental work can be done by anyone on the floor. Learning is done in real time, and more skilled mechanics teach the newer recruits. The result is a bay that can be managed by skill set.

We look for every opportunity to find these groups in organizations. This includes programming, project management, accounting, legal, and human resources, to name a few.

Standardization of Work Outputs

When all the other approaches fail to be useful, we resort to using output measures as a means of coordination.

This is where we need to pause in our look at structure. Every part of the organization, regardless of how the work is coordinated, needs to have output measures. We don't simply trust that the groups that are being managed by processes or skills or even mutual adjustment are doing a great job. We verify with output measures. *However,* there is a big difference between having output measures to ensure performance and using output measures to actually coordinate work.

We resort to an output standardization when we know what the outcomes of the work effort should be but don't know precisely how each employee should ideally reach that outcome. Consider store clerks. They greet you, help you pick out the item or service that you are looking for, process your sale, and wish you a great day. We have all had experiences with folks who do a great job and folks who do a bad job. Some people want to chat, other people just want the facts, and others need their hand held along the way. There is no one way to sell in a store. Customer service centers are another example where we know we want a satisfied customer who doesn't take too long with one of our reps, while not requiring too many additional resources. Yet there are all types of service representative models that work and work well (not to mention the companies that have turned this area into one of their competitive advantages).

The key to this type of coordination is the crafting of the output metrics. They have to be designed in such a way that we attain the performance that we are trying to achieve. We want the store clerk to be friendly, but how much time do we want that person to spend with each customer? We want to sell as many items to a single customer as we can, but how far do we push the customer before he or she is "turned off"? We want the stock to remain refreshed and well organized, but not at the cost of making a customer wait at the register. When we are using output measures to coordinate the work, senior management is examining the results of those output measures to infer whether an employee is effective.

While sales is a classic example of an area where output measures are particularly effective, so can the business analysis area, the on-site child development center, the reception area, and many more. If you can develop an effective way to use processes or skills to manage a group, then you will only need output measures to *evaluate* their effectiveness. If you must move to output as a means of coordination, then you will have to craft an extensive list of measures to *ensure* effectiveness (keeping in mind that mutual adjustment only works in very limited circumstances).

Standardization of Business Norms

At the beginning of this chapter, we stated that there was a fifth means of work coordination that was still being debated. A standardization of business norms suggests that everyone in the organization understands and fully embraces a "company norm" that acts as a means of worker coordination. This approach to coordination suggests that a well-developed set of "norms" would guide everyone to do the right thing. This is the focus of the so-called structureless companies.

While this has been seen in a number of smaller companies where the founder(s) can constantly reiterate and train employees in the norms of the business, it has not been effectively instituted in a larger organization (although some have claimed that they operate this way). Regardless of the approach, desire, or direction of the business, it is very difficult to provide sufficient context to make this approach work effectively. There are so many nuances to every aspect of a position within a company that require the constant reinforcing of norms that it becomes impractical except in the most unusual circumstances.

There are some companies that have brushed close to this approach, but they did so at a significant cost. That cost is probably well worth it in innovative or groundbreaking areas of business. One of the longest-lasting companies to get close to this approach is W. L. Gore (maker of Gore-Tex). There are structures at the company including senior management, divisions, and product-focused groups, but they try to keep units under two hundred people so that there can be direct interaction with every member of the team (called "associates" at Gore).[7] The newest large company to move in this direction is Zappos. Instituting what is being called a "holacracy," they are attempting to achieve the same thing as W. L. Gore and the promise of moving closer to a standardization of norms.

The hope and promise of this approach is probably not in its pure implementation, but in the effort to reduce layers of management, speed up decision making, and improve the contact with the customer. All of those are laudable goals that don't require coordination experimentation or risking the future of the company to achieve.

All of these elements (the three areas of the business and the coordinating method utilized) are then put into a structure form that makes sense to the executive management of the business. These forms were briefly mentioned at the beginning of the chapter (functional, geographic, multidomestic, etc.) in order to keep the company focused on doing the standard elements of the business well while expanding the competitive advantages of the business.

---

7 Garry Hamel, "Innovation Democracy: W. L. Gore's Original Management Model," *Management Information Exchange*, September 23, 2010, accessed August 25, 2014, http://www.managementexchange.com/story/innovation-democracy-wl-gores-original-management-model.

Chapter 10

ALIGNMENT AND THE ONE-PAGE STRATEGY IMPLEMENTATION MAP

Bringing everything together into a workable strategic plan has been an issue since the birth of management as a field of study. Regardless of how the strategy of the business was developed, communicating that to every employee in a manner that is continually reinforced is quite difficult. Strategic plans earned their classic bad name from the fact that they

- Had little to do with the actual operation of the business
- Were never reviewed by senior management after being put into place
- Were ponderous documents bound in huge three-ring binders
- Wasted untold hours of time in their development
- Often were little more than incremental works that were primarily used for budget purposes

None of that is strategy, and it is certainly not the way to implement strategy.

Various attempts have been made to rectify this situation. Some companies mandated that their plans be limited in size, causing all kinds of consternation and eight-point font reports by lower-level managers worried about being held accountable without being able to explain the details. Approaches like the balanced scorecard came and went, leaving more of a bad taste than actually accomplishing anything of value. The concepts around the balanced scorecard were fine; the form was ineffective. Thinking about strategy is good, designing a real strategy is better, and actually implementing that strategy is amazing.

The approach to strategy implementation outlined in this chapter has been used quite successfully in many industries and across different-sized organizations. It has been around in roughly this form since the early 2000s and allows the entire strategy to be laid out on a single page or screen. If you search the Internet for strategy maps, you will see examples of this in various forms. The sophistication of the approach can be mind-boggling (little avatars climbing ladders). In this chapter we will look at the fundamentals and a very straightforward template for doing this within your company.

A key point to this is to decide how many maps will be needed in the organization. There should be only *one* map for the entire company. Unfortunately, the reality is that many companies are too complex for that. While there can and should be an overall map for the whole organization, there may be a need for individual areas to have their own maps.

The best rule of thumb that we have seen is to create a separate map whenever the competitive set or perfect customer is significantly different. These two elements are the foundation for the strategy that is ultimately designed. If they differ substantially from group to group, then each group will need to craft their own map. Therefore, even though we show maps for overall organizations here and in the appendix, recognize that most organizations have many maps that must be tied together into a coherent strategy.

Another key tenet of great strategy implementation is that everyone in the organization understands what the strategy is, how it will be measured (the metrics that you will use), what they can do to impact the strategy, and what the company will do to support them trying to implement the strategy. Large, convoluted, and difficult to understand "strategies" may look impressive to analysts, but they will not accomplish the real goal of strategy implementation.

Implementation is accomplished by everyone in the organization. Effective implementation is about fit and alignment within the company such that the customer receives a consistent experience that is focused on those elements that truly provide the company a competitive advantage. The strategy map below (and as seen earlier) has a number of elements:

Header Line

Perfect Customer—A short description of the perfect customer.

Comparison Set—The list of four or five companies that constitute our comparison competitive set.

Standard Operations—A short list of the big standard elements of the business that constitute the table stakes for the business.

@Copyright 2015 by Charles E. Bamford

The core part of the map consists of five columns:

Value Driver—All the resource-based advantages are listed in this column.

Stakeholder Statements—Each value driver is translated into statements we would like to hear from customers, competitors, suppliers, or other relevant stakeholders.

Need from the Company—What must be done at the company level in order to achieve the statements that we have listed in column 2?

Must Do Individually—What can be done *now* by the individual employee to help achieve the statements listed in column 2? This is the only column that changes from person to person in the company.

Metrics—How will success be measured at the company level?

The strategy map is simply a way to bring together all the work from this book in a format that is easy to use on a daily basis. While the elements of the strategy map are fairly straightforward, it is worth taking some time to examine the individual elements.

Value Driver

Let's start with the core part of the map. The current or new resource-based advantages (RBA) should be listed in the first column. A key to doing this well is to craft the RBA into a succinct but meaningful set of words. If we go back to the fast-food restaurant we discussed in the previous chapter, you might remember that the two RBAs were as follows:

1) A 24-7 operation where the customer can have breakfast or regular food items anytime, and
2) A private dining area where no cell phone may be used and where no talking is allowed.

We might recraft these into value drivers that state the following:

1) Any food, any time
2) Quiet room

The goal is to message the essence of the RBA such that everyone in the organization knows the basic approach.

The problem with short concepts is that they often are not sufficiently descriptive. We get RBAs such as the following:

1) Customer is first
2) Widest offering
3) Fifteen-minute guarantee
4) Transformational operations
5) Innovative cost management
6) Distributed decisions

If something like these exist, the strategy implementation effort must be refined to get underneath these big concepts to what really constitutes the underlying competitive advantages.

Stakeholder Statements

Each of these concepts needs to be expanded so that every employee knows what the executives meant when they crafted the term—we want to reduce variation in the interpretation by employees. The method that seems to work the best is to convert these concepts into statements that we would want customers, competitors, or even governmental officials to say about the organization relative to that specific value driver.

While there is no perfect statement, we do want something that could actually be said.

For our fictional fast-food restaurant, we might develop stakeholder statements for each value driver that state the following:

1) Any food, any time
   a. Customer statements
      i. "I love being able to eat breakfast at night."

      ii. "A burger at eight in the morning is just what the doctor ordered."

  b. Competitor statements

      i. "It's just too hard to set up lunch food when we are serving breakfast."

      ii. "No one has ever asked us for eggs at midnight."

2) Quiet room

  a. Customer statements

      i. "Finally, peace and quiet when I have to eat in a hurry."

      ii. "Glad that I don't bother anyone now with the calls I have to take during lunch."

  b. Competitor statements

      i. "I wouldn't want to offend our customers like that."

      ii. "No one comes here for quiet time."

The goal is to help the employees see more specifically what each competitive advantage is hoping to accomplish. If customers were to make one of these statements, then they might drive right past our competitors.

Need from the Company

In order for the company to start moving toward the statements we want to hear from customers and competitors, there are usually a number of overarching company efforts that must be in place. These are the crucial elements that the company needs to do if they want to implement their strategy. In our fast-food example, these might be as follows:

1) Develop procedures for ensuring that quiet rooms remain quiet

2) Build quiet room facilities in each location

3) Develop processes and training to deliver all offered food items 24-7

4) Change out all menu boards to reflect new offering
5) Change supply stock to reflect varying demand for products offered

Metrics

As we covered extensively in chapter 8, the development of strategy metrics is a crucial part of the implementation process. We want to know what will constitute success before we implement a strategy. The metrics need to be specific to the element (value driver and statement) being evaluated.

There is a big difference between the metrics that are used in a strategy map and those used to measure the overall performance of the company (or part of the company covered by the map). While we want to know how the overall company is performing (ROI, net profit margin, free cash flow, market share, etc.), in the strategy map we are trying to evaluate *activities* so that we can be sure that the strategy itself is being implemented. If we are right about the direction of the strategy *and* if it is actually being implemented (no small feat), then the company performance measures should move up post hoc (viewing and analyzing the data after the effort has been expended).

In this instance, the strategy map measures might include the following:

1) Percentage of locations with quiet rooms (we want this to go up)
2) Number of minutes that the quiet rooms were used by patrons (we want this to go up)
2) Number of minutes when quiet rooms were disturbed by store location (we want this to go down)
3) Number of "breakfast" items sold outside 6:00 a.m. to 10:30 a.m. (we would like to see this go up)
4) Percentage of orders per hour per store that are nontraditional orders (we would like to see this go up)

As each of these measures moves in the direction that senior management would like to see, we can presume that the strategy is being more and more implemented in the field—these results imply that we are on the right track. Over the same period of time, we would like to see all those classic financial measures of performance increase.

Life is good when the financial measures of performance increase as our strategy (activity) metrics move in the desired directions. We can be confident that the strategy is effective.

The strategy is flawed when we see the financial measures of performance decrease as our strategy (activity) metrics move in the desired directions. The strategy is being implemented by the employees, but it is not having a positive effect on our overall performance. We are spending time, energy, and resources and not getting a gain.

The strategy is not being implemented if we see the strategy metrics not moving in the desired direction, whether or not financial measures of performance increase or decrease. Changes in financial performance are simply a result of random events and activities that are not being coordinated.

Must Do Individually

You will note that we saved column 4 for last. This column is filled out by every employee individually in answer to the question "What can I do *now* to make this happen?" It is incumbent on each manager to ensure that the strategy document is personalized. Every employee has a role to play in this effort. Even if most of the employee's job involves the standard part of the business, it is important for each person to articulate how and where he or she can contribute to the strategy of the business. This is best done with a conversation and then a tie to the performance review of the employee.

Implementation Process

Once the map has been designed, the process of personalizing each person's map should start at the top. The most senior executive in the organization should fill out what he or she can do now to make each value driver a reality. That person's map should then be handed to each of his or her direct reports. After those people have filled their parts of the map out, then they should use that to have a discussion with their manager before handing it to their direct reports. The process continues until everyone in the organization has completed his or her own map. It is a cascading model that really pushes for a *fit* in the whole organization.

The overall strategy map outlines the key competitive advantages of the organization. Converting that into an operational plan is an important step. Conceptually, we view the process as follows:

Each resource-based advantage should be developed into a project plan that ties to the strategy map. While there are many variations on project plans and project plan approaches, it is important to ensure that the activities tie directly to the strategy being pursued.

Appendix

EXAMPLE STRATEGY MAPS

It seems valuable to look at a few examples of strategy maps for some organizations. These have been crafted by my students in various executive classes for real companies as a way of applying the technique outside their own organizations (safer that way). The students had no contact with the real companies and these were completed with only publicly available information. They are not from the actual companies and any actual resemblence to the strategies being considered by those companies would be coincidence. Unfortunately, I am not able to provide the actual strategy maps of my clients for obvious reasons. I've modified these maps in order to make them more applicable to the reader.

In each case I've made notes about what would improve the effort.

Intel TV Strategy Map

KEY VALUE DRIVER	STAKEHOLDER STATEMENTS	NEED FROM COMPANY	MUST DO	KEY METRICS
Customizable/ Adaptable	"Intel gives me all of the channels that I want and none of the ones that I don't" "Intel gives me the best ideas for shows that I didn't even know about!" "I can't believe all the different options Intel has." "I can pinpoint my perfect customer with Intel TV."	• *Capability to mix/match channels in every combination* • *"Genius" Program for recommendations based on viewing* • *Precise Advertising algorithms that can be customized for distribution*	*What I must do to make this happen*	• # of shows chosen from suggestion menu • % of revenue generated from up-selling • Advertising revenues per user • # of channels available
Social Connection	"Intel TV is the place to be." "Watching Intel TV is like having all of my friends from across the country in my living room." "I have found the three other people who like XYZ show. Watching it together, we can geek out."	• *Develop a seamless social networking add-on* • *Possible tie to existing social networking apps operating in real-time*	*What I must do to make this happen*	• % of market share • # of new connections per user per month • # of channel adds based on other reviewer recommendations • # of interactions per show

This strategy map gets right to the two resource-based advantages that the group believes Intel TV has over the competition. In a separate file, they listed the following:

Comparative competitive set: Direct TV, Comcast, and AT&T

Standard operations:

- Offer a static viewing experience with no interaction capabilities
- Tiered service offerings
- Live feed only

It is better to list the competitors, the perfect customer, and the big standard operations elements as part of the map, as this is what most employees will have in hand. Understanding the common playing field is important to understanding the strategy.

Note also that the team lists "percentage of market share" as a metric. While we might want to see market share increase (depending on what other metrics were considered important), the fact remains that market share is an outcome metric and not a strategy implementation metric. It is not action oriented and does not provide any direction to employees. While the choice of metrics is always a matter of opinion, we would like to separate post hoc measures from strategy action measures. As was stated earlier in the book, we always want to see post hoc results that improve; they are just not a part of the strategy map.

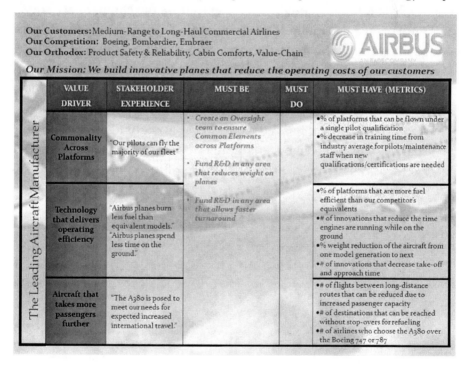

Our Customers: Medium-Range to Long-Haul Commercial Airlines
Our Competition: Boeing, Bombardier, Embraer
Our Orthodox: Product Safety & Reliability, Cabin Comforts, Value-Chain

Our Mission: We build innovative planes that reduce the operating costs of our customers

	VALUE DRIVER	STAKEHOLDER EXPERIENCE	MUST BE	MUST DO	MUST HAVE (METRICS)
The Leading Aircraft Manufacturer	Commonality Across Platforms	"Our pilots can fly the majority of our fleet"	*Create an Oversight team to ensure Common Elements across Platforms* *Fund R&D in any area that reduces weight on planes*		•% of platforms that can be flown under a single pilot qualification •% decrease in training time from industry average for pilots/maintenance staff when new qualifications/certifications are needed
	Technology that delivers operating efficiency	"Airbus planes burn less fuel than equivalent models." "Airbus planes spend less time on the ground."	*Fund R&D in any area that allows faster turnaround*		•% of platforms that are more fuel efficient than our competitor's equivalents •# of innovations that reduce the time engines are running while on the ground •% weight reduction of the aircraft from one model generation to next •# of innovations that decrease take-off and approach time
	Aircraft that takes more passengers further	"The A380 is posed to meet our needs for expected increased international travel."			•# of flights between long-distance routes that can be reduced due to increased passenger capacity •# of destinations that can be reached without stop-overs for refueling •# of airlines who choose the A380 over the Boeing 747 or 787

This strategy map has headers that list out the position of the company. The only questionable issue might be the inclusion of "value chain" as an orthodox element. I'm not sure what is meant here, and if it is not obvious to the employees, then it should not be in the map.

Furthermore, few areas of a business are more ripe for creating true competitive advantages than the value chain of the business.

In this case the focus is clearly on the commercial aircraft arm of Airbus. Note that the mission is not one that the company currently uses but one that the students felt fit the true competitive advantages that they were trying to achieve.

The resource-based advantages (value drivers) are all geared toward the elements that the students believed separated the company from its competitors. The statements are directly aimed at the value drivers and are simple and understandable. The needs from the company are aimed at improving the capability of the business to deliver on its value drivers.

The metrics for the first value driver are specific to the goals desired, as are the metrics for the second value driver. Each of these metrics aims to focus the efforts of employees on the element that is desired. The metrics for the third value driver seem to be more post hoc measures. They observe what happens afterward to get at the statement. The only one that has a leading-edge element to it is the second metric, but even that metric is only loosely aimed at the goal of the value driver. Put bigger fuel tanks on the plane, and it can fly around the world?

Strategy Map

Perfect Customer: Tech savvy; willing to pay more for luxury, quality, control, efficiency, and convenience

Competitive Set: Taxi cabs, limo services, and personal car transportation services

Industry Orthodox: On-demand means of transportation

Value Drivers	Stakeholder Experiences (Statements)	Need From the Company	Must Do Individually	Metrics
Convenience	No tipping or exchanging money – what could be easier!?! All of I have to do is launch an app and I have a ride. Easy to cancel my ride if I'm uncomfortable.	Investment in app (headcount & technology), proper screening of drivers & cars, sales & marketing (headcount & advertising), customer service (surveys & results), and enforcement of policies & metrics	What must I do to make this happen?	• # repeat customers citing convenience • Customer survey marks for utility & convenience of app • Frequency of ride cancellations due to driver or car
Reassurance	I'm never late I feel like I have more control over my travel I like having no surprises!			• % of on-time pickups • Customer survey marks citing assurance as important • # errors pertaining to ride info for travelers
Professionalism	I love being able to rate the driver & my experience! More like a chauffeur than a driver Great service – the car was clean & luxurious!			• # of 4 or 5 star ratings for cleanliness & service • # of Customer surveys • # repeat, referred customers citing cleanliness & service

Uber has been an interesting business to watch develop. The students did a nice job pitching the Uber competitive advantages and how the business can compete. The whole map works pretty well, is focused on the unique elements of the business, and provides management with direction and measures of performance.

About the Author

Dr. Chuck Bamford is the managing partner of Bamford Associates, a firm focused on developing practical strategic plans and working with companies to implement those plans throughout the organization.

Before earning his PhD, Bamford spent twelve years in industry. For the past twenty years, he has taught strategy and entrepreneurship at the undergraduate, graduate, and executive levels. He is currently an adjunct professor at the University of Notre Dame and has won eighteen teaching excellence awards, including nine executive MBA Professor of the YearAwards and has been named a Noble Foundation Fellow in Teaching Excellence.

Bamford is the author of five textbooks in both Strategy and Entrepreneurship. His research studies have appeared in the top journals of both fields and he regularly contributes to news organizations.

CPSIA information can be obtained at www.ICGtesting.com
Printed in the USA
LVOW10s2335120615

442318LV00012B/81/P